The Planned Giving Idea Book

The
Planned Giving
Idea Book

Robert F. Sharpe

THOMAS NELSON PUBLISHERS
Nashville

5/326

Second printing, updated, 1980

Library of Congress Cataloging in Publication Data

Sharpe, Robert.
  The planned giving idea book.

  Includes index.
  1. Charities—United States. 2. Charitable bequests—United States. 3. Endowments—United States. 4. Charitable uses, trusts and foundations—United States. I. Title.
HV40.S55   361.7'6'0973   78-10708
  ISBN 0-8407-4068-9

To Jane

Contents

List of Tables

Acknowledgments

This book could not have been written without the help of Selva Roark Rorabaugh, who invested many hours editing, writing, and rewriting the manuscript. She is a "possibility person." What I have considered impossible for years, she has made possible. I am indebted to her.

Mrs. Rorabaugh received editorial assistance from Judi Simpson and Betty Gee.

The first serious attempt to write this book came about three years ago when I took a week off and came up with an outline and two rough chapters. I thank Gail and Jane White for inviting me to use their home while they were vacationing so these seeds could germinate.

David Stone, who kindly wrote the book's foreword, was responsible for building a fire under me by asking at the completion of his seminar experience, "When are you going to write a book?" He helped bring the publisher and myself together.

Philip Ray Converse, LL.B., my associate for the last six years, has read the manuscript and made many contributions, both legal and otherwise. Also, his chapters add significantly to the overall completeness of this book.

My longtime friends, E. Fred Alexander, Charles H. Branch, Theodore W. Hurst, Rod Sargent, Ralph W. Sanders, and Franklin Robbie contributed much to the book, and I am grateful.

My sons, Bob, Paul, and Tim Sharpe, did the hard work of indexing and preparing the glossary. I am indebted to them for their team effort and the expeditious completion of this demanding task. My daughter, Sue, and my wife, Jane, double-checked the galleys and gave me invaluable help.

Elizabeth Houston came out of retirement to type, type, and retype this manuscript. Dot Walker and Bo McElroy assisted her.

I didn't know how much sheer enjoyment there could be in writing a book. It has been an enriching experience to work with the editors, Pete Gillquist, Larry Stone, and Bruce Nygren.

Finally, there are the "teachers." The experiences I have had with institutional managers have taught me much, and I have had great fun while helping many people give. There are many, many people to whom I am indebted; to name them all would considerably lengthen this book.

I am especially indebted to a few very good friends who had the patience to hear me out in several almost one-sided conversations. They listened as I talked about my ideas and dreams of how a book like this could help institutional managers think through how more income can be given to their institutions so that their work can become a joy rather than a constant problem.

Thanks to one . . . thanks to all.

R.F.S.

Foreword

I received my first formal training in the field of planned giving at a week-long seminar conducted by Bob Sharpe. Several things impressed me at that first seminar. First, as I got to know my fellow students, I realized what a broad range of organizations were interested in planned giving. The participants in the seminar represented institutions which work in the fields of religion, education, medicine, and social services. Second, the amount of money which is given each year in the United States for charitable purposes is enormous, amounting to many billions of dollars. My fellow students were talking of substantial sums when they discussed their giving programs. Finally, many rules by which the business world operates do not apply to charitable giving. The charitable giver is not motivated by the desire for financial profit. His motivation is the satisfaction he receives in meeting the needs of the world about him. The role of government in charitable giving is one of encouragement. It induces philanthropy by providing tax relief according to carefully defined procedures.

Because planned giving is so vital to the survival of many worthy enterprises and involves so many unique aspects, an authoritative source of information about it is needed. This book is that authority. A book on planned giving must cover the mechanics of many giving vehicles and programs, and the author has done this well. A second phase of the book is a presentation of successful methods which have actually been used in planned giving programs. The twenty years of experience which he has had in this field give Bob Sharpe a wealth of material. He has approached his subject not only as a qualified expert, and he is that, but also as an unusually successful practitioner. When he speaks of methods that work and those that do not, he speaks with the experience of one who has analyzed both and can explain the difference in results.

In that first seminar with Bob Sharpe, I also realized how diversified were the backgrounds of the members of our student body. Would it be possible for our instructor to present his subject matter in such a way that it would be readily comprehensible to all of us? Our group included ordained clergymen, professional educators, salesmen, and many types of businessmen and women. As our seminar progressed the material was clearly understood by those who were new to the field and offered a challenge to the more experienced students. This gift of teaching has been carried over into this book. Readers with an interest in the subject will find the book easily understandable and most profitable—whatever their former contact with this field of study.

This book provides background in legal and mathematical phases of planned giving, but its value is much more than that. It also provides the person who wants to establish a planned giving program with the step-by-step procedure for developing the program. The appendixes give suggested documents to be used in the program. Case studies from the author's own experience give life and reality to the subject. After reading the book, I felt as though an expert in the field had led me by the hand. We had avoided the hazards and pitfalls along the way and had arrived at our desired destination. For the person with a will to be successful in planned giving, this book provides the way.

David G. Stone, Ph.D.
Former President
Stone, Young & Company,
Consulting Actuaries

Preface

If I had it to do all over again, I would.

My career in the field of financial development generally, and planned giving in particular, began in 1959 and is still going. During these years, I have helped provide many millions of dollars for good causes. Of course, there have been frustrating times, but for the most part I have experienced real joy in helping donors satisfy their need to give by assisting them in aiding the institutions of their choice.

But I know many men, and a few women, who have abandoned planned giving as a vocation and have gone back to teaching, or back into a pastorate, or back into business, because planned giving as a career was not working for them, at least not fast enough. And besides, their mothers-in-law could never figure out what they were doing and kept calling it "fund raising."

One statistic says that eighteen months is the average career life expectancy for development officers for charitable causes.

I know of chief executive officers who have toyed with the idea of the "larger gift" program for their institutions. They looked at donor lists, shuffled cards, sent out mailings, made a dozen phone calls . . . and nothing happened. It just seemed a dead-end street. They felt there wasn't time or money available to explore such a program. The "we-need-cash-*now*" crunch got to them, and they gave up on planned giving.

On the other hand, I have worked with several hundred

planned giving officers who have discovered what I call the "Big Idea" about planned giving, and they as well as their institutions have "made it." These men and women have become involved in helping people fulfill their own need to give, have helped them plan, and have done a commendable, irreplaceable service to their institutions, while having the time of their lives.

What makes the difference? Why do some planned giving officers succeed and others so soundly fail? Why are some institutions annually receiving gifts through wills as a substantial source of income, while others see only a rare bequest? Why are some institutions always hurting for cash and sending out continual crisis appeals, while others seem to prosper beyond their needs?

The practical steps in this book offer an answer to such questions. I believe most of the people who have failed as planned giving officers did not have to fail. With careful career selection, adequate financial backing, proper training, and a lot of patience, I believe most could have succeeded. Institutions rendering a valid service to society can do much to secure their future through planned giving. They don't have to plead with their donors from crisis to crisis.

When I started in this field, planned giving was new to most institutions. Many had never heard of a revocable trust and were suspicious of gift annuities. There were not any annuity trusts, unitrusts, or pooled income funds as we know them today. Most charities *could* tolerate gifts through wills but didn't have a good plan for getting them.

There are some painful memories. Thinking back twenty years, I recall how I talked with board members and administrative personnel of the first institution I worked for and watched them juggle budget allowances to squeeze out one more mailing. Meanwhile, I was wondering if Mrs. Rogers would actually sign the final contract for a living trust with our organization. "Can I justify my own salary?" I would ask myself. "And the huge telephone expenses? Are the coast-to-coast air trips necessary? When, if ever, will we see the first will probated? Will it be in time to save our program?"

I really struggled with these problems while supporting my wife and four children. I simply *had* to succeed—or quit and go back to selling life insurance.

What I learned first through the trial and error and success method, and later as a professional consultant, I have had the opportunity to pass along in person through the National Planned Giving Institute, which began ten years ago. The Institute offers a training program consisting of eight seminars in planned giving, financial development, and management. The seminars cover how to start a planned giving program; how to attract and manage bequests, gifts of life insurance, securities, revocable living trusts, charitable remainder trusts, gift annuities, and other gifts-for-income; and how all this fits into the total financial development program of the institution. We discuss capital campaigns, foundation and corporation gifts, memorial giving, other special gift sources, direct mail techniques, and public relations.

I have never tried to put this information into a book until now. When I was learning the ropes firsthand, there weren't many books on the subject. If you're the kind of person who likes to learn things firsthand and you have twenty years to invest yourself—go to it, and blessings on you.

My objective in writing this book is to convey to the management of not-for-profit institutions an understanding of how to start a new planned giving program, or how to build an existing one that will help people give more effectively—a program that will build a bridge to the future while securing the present financial base of the institution.

Numerous institutions with five- to ten-year-old giving programs are now receiving an occasional substantial gift as a result of their consistent public relations and interviewing efforts. Even as I write this, one of our clients, with a program less than three years old, has just received $270,000 from a will written by a person who had received a direct mail promotion on wills from this institution. Another institution reports receiving nearly one million dollars from only two estates. *In both cases these bequests amounted to almost as much as their annual gift budget!* Both institutions are also ahead in goals for current gifts to date.

One other word: About forty percent of my life has been spent helping people give away their money and other property to institutions that are doing a work they believe in. My experience and observations tell me that *giving* really is a blessed way to live.* I hope I can help you help others with their giving so your institution can continue to carry out its mission without financial crisis.

Robert F. Sharpe

Robert F. Sharpe and Co., Inc.
5050 Poplar Avenue
Memphis, Tennessee 38157

*Acts 20:35, New Testament.

Chapter One
Helping the Giver Give

Tom and Sarah served as loyal volunteers for many years with a charitable organization. When Tom died, Sarah continued to serve with great dedication. One day she called the institution's headquarters to say she had found an old life insurance policy of Tom's. She had thought it was of no value, but it had paid off and now she had some funds she wanted to use for the work of the mission in Tom's memory.

The board of trustees was prepared to handle such matters, and the planned giving director helped her with information and paperwork. A substantial improvement of the institution's property was arranged—to the loving memory of Tom, a faithful volunteer.

What this gift did for that institution was outstanding for its material provision alone. What it did in inspiring others to personal dedication and generous giving was also commendable. But what it did for Sarah was best of all. It satisfied her need to give and to honor the memory of her beloved partner. And that's what makes the planned giving officer's job satisfying, although not every gift comes wrapped up in such loving concern.

Four Kinds of Givers

To better understand what motivates people to share their material means, let's take a look at four types of givers.

The impulsive giver is one whose giving is strictly spontane-

19

ous. I believe this is the way most people give. The problem with this kind of giver is that if he doesn't give when the impulse comes, he may not give at all. It is not that he doesn't want to give, but rather that he has other stronger impulses.

For example, when he receives a stirring challenge to give, he may have neither cash nor a blank check. As he drives home he receives many other impulses—to buy a new rug, trade cars, buy a new suit of clothes, or use the money for savings. If the institution wants to correct the problem of not receiving these important impulsive gifts, it must come up with new vehicles or methods for giving.

The banking industry has established and installed new ways to carry on its business. First, the credit card. Then, computer-depositing and -withdrawing of money. One such system in my hometown is called *Annie*. You can make your deposits and withdrawals by punching in code numbers on a small computer console. Nonprofit institutions need to use this kind of technology and make it possible for people to "punch in" their gifts to them in the same way they "punch in" banking transactions. A study of the feasibility of such a plan by the nonprofit sector is long overdue. Why must we tag behind and be the last to use computer technology to help people give?

The habitual giver gives as a routine. Recently, after attending the Sunday morning worship service at my church, a good friend asked, "Where did you sit?"

I told her, "In the back of the church, but I didn't see your husband or you."

She said, "He was mad this morning because someone else got his regular seat and we had to sit elsewhere."

Jokingly I asked, "Does he hang his hat and coat on the same rack in the same place every Sunday?"

"How did you know?" she responded.

This fellow also parks his car in the same place every Sunday. And a study would probably indicate that he is very much a person of habit in other areas. I know nothing of his giving habits, but I am almost certain he will give the same amount, at the same time, to the same institutions by habit and without much prompting. It would be difficult to motivate him to upgrade his giving. But the habitual giver is important to the ongoing work of any institution because he is *dependable*.

The thoughtful giver reasons things out before he gives. He considers the need of one institution versus another. "Why should I give now?" he may think. Or, "Should I give to the Red Cross, the United Way, or both?" This type of giver is part of a minority—perhaps representing less than ten percent of all givers— but he is extremely important in securing funds for the overall budget.

A man we'll call Dr. Jones is a professor of economics at a large university. His total income is almost $47,000 a year from all sources. He gives away about $5,000 each year. For three years he gave to the small college he attended some thirty years ago. He told me, "I can't give much to any institution if I spread it around to every charity making an appeal. I prefer to give to only one or two places at a time."

Dr. Jones gave $15,000 over three years to his alma mater because it was starting a new program that he thought was vital to the future of the college. He was deeply interested in other institutions, but after thinking it through he decided his college had the projects he wanted to support. He mentioned to me his feeling that he should support this new program at the college because it would be difficult for the rank-and-file donor to identify with the program and thus be motivated to give as he was. Dr. Jones is a thoughtful giver.

The careful giver is the most valuable giver. While I cannot prove this statistically, I believe that less than three percent of all givers give carefully. It has been my experience that this type of person investigates the institution before he gives. He may ask serious but valid questions, such as: What part of your gifts go into administration or fund raising costs? Who are you as an institution? What is your mission? Whose work are you duplicating? Is your existence really necessary? How will you use my gift? What will happen if you don't receive my gift? What are your plans for the future? Send me a copy of your audited financial statement. Tell me about salaries and your employment practices.

Several years ago a person I worked with told me he had

inherited a substantial amount of property from his mother. He was giving to thirteen organizations at that time. He told me he had been deeply disappointed in giving and wondered how he could investigate these institutions. Finally, we drew up twenty-two key questions, and not wanting to use his name, he asked me to send a list of these to each of the institutions he was supporting financially. (See this questionnaire on pages 185–186.)

This questionnaire was sent to all thirteen institutions. Ten of them answered all the questions as best they could. The three others didn't feel they wanted to send this kind of information to me without knowing who would receive it. The ten institutions answering the questions each received approximately $30,000. The three institutions not answering the questions received nothing. If you want larger gifts of money from the public, you must be open to the public.

As you build a comprehensive financial development program in your institution, I believe you must do your work and make your plans as though all of your giving friends are *careful givers*.

Three Kinds of Money

People give three kinds of money. Harold Stephens, a fund raising consultant and long-time stewardship officer for the Moody Bible Institute in Chicago, once made note of this in a speech to a group of development officers: "There is outright gift money, investment gift money, and bequest gift money."

Outright Gift Money is money or other property I can give *now*. I completely divest myself of its use *now*, and the institution can use the money *now*. People give not only cash but also stocks, bonds, notes, leases, farms, houses, life insurance, crops, animals, and works of art. I heard of a dairy farmer who had sixty cows. He gave the proceeds from the sale of the milk from six cows to support a mission project.

I have served as a consultant to a boys' ranch. This institution has a truck that travels throughout the countryside receiving gifts of young calves. Cattle-raising is a vital part of the work projects for the boys. What rancher could resist giving a calf to help restore a wayward boy? Don't forget to think in terms of gifts other than cash. Invite people to give what they have. The late president of Wheaton College, Dr. J. Oliver Buswell, once told me, "Find out what a person owns and ask him to give one of them. If he has seven factories, ask him for one of them."

Investment Gift Money is money or other property I can give only if it provides me with an income for my lifetime or some period of years. When a person places money in a gift annuity or a trust, or retains a life estate—providing your institution with the remainder interest at death—he in effect gives because you provided him with a needed income. Many substantial gifts of this kind are missed by many institutions simply because they have not made it known that they want such gifts and are prepared to manage them.

One donor wrote to a well-known charitable institution and offered $25,000 for a gift annuity. The management responded that the institution did not take such gifts and referred the person to one of our client institutions. Today, that first institution has its own fully staffed planned giving program.

Bequest Gift Money is money or other property a person *can't* give now. He or she cannot give it even if you provide a life income. This person can only give it when the money is no longer needed—at death. Such money comes through the person's will.

Although it seems odd, it is important to realize that many people do not name your institutions in their wills simply because they do not know you can accept their gifts.

During 1977, 6.0 percent of the income received through gifts by American nonprofit organizations came from wills. Therefore, it is imperative that we make every effort to take advantage of this significant source of income. In 1977, gifts from bequests exceeded gifts from all American foundations, which gave 5.7 percent of the total.[1]

[1]Donald R. Hannum, *Giving U.S.A.*, American Association of Fund-Raising Counsel, 1978 Annual Report (New York, N.Y.), p. 6.

Three Purposes for Gifts

People give money to nonprofit institutions for three basic purposes: (1) for day-to-day operations, (2) for capital improvements, and (3) for endowment.

The make-up of some people is such that they will give for any or all of the above purposes. They, in effect, say, "Here is my gift. Use it when and where you want to." Others do not want to build buildings or establish endowments, but will give to cover operating expenses. Some are known as "brick and mortar" people and like to give for buildings. They like to *see* how their money is used. Then a few like to take a long, hard look at our institutions and put their money into endowments so their giving can continue for many future years. Endowment income can become the foundation of many annual budgets since only the income from the gift is used by the institution.

Since people give for these various purposes, it is essential that we go to the trouble to learn just what the interests of the individual really are and then try to fit our need for gifts to his interest in giving. This cannot be done with every donor, but it should be a primary consideration as we work with our larger donors or prospective donors.

Planned givers whom we approach through a wills and bequest program are usually in the careful-giver category. They give through wills and often through contracts for all three purposes, but especially for endowment.

Now we are ready to move on and take a closer look at this comparatively untapped resource for charitable causes— *planned giving.*

Chapter Two
Where Does Planned
Giving Fit In?

One of the first planned gifts in this country predated the birth of the nation by some 138 years. It was the bequest that helped launch the first American institution of higher education. Rev. John Harvard in 1638 bequeathed to Cambridge College eight hundred pounds and three hundred books, a bequest worthy of renaming the college in honor of this benefactor.[1] (Other gifts and bequests to this institution at that time included sheep, a pewter flagon worth one hundred shillings, and a half bushel of corn!)

A Brief History of Giving

The responsibility for taking care of those in need has been felt for a long time. The Hammurabic Code of 2000 B.C. told the ancient Babylonians to see that "justice be done to widows, orphans, and the poor."

In 1300 B.C. the children of Israel gave tithes for the support of their religion and the relief of the needy. Their laws made ample provision for strangers and the poor of their land.

The early Christian church had its common fund for care of widows and others in need. These efforts were gradually organized into special ministries to the sick, the orphans and widows, the poor, and the strangers. Support for hospitals

---

[1]Historical information in this section is drawn from Joseph Nathan Kane, *Famous First Facts* (New York: H. W. Wilson, 1950) and Arnaud C. Marts, *Man's Concern for His Fellow-Man* (Geneva, N.Y.: Marts & Lundy, 1961).

flourished during the Middle Ages, as did "scholasticism" for the preservation and enlargement of knowledge— foreshadowing the development of universities in western Europe.

Early American interest in charitable works stemmed from European roots. Strong support was given to such works by English bankers and merchants who used not only direct giving but also bequests and charitable trusts.

Clara Barton founded the first organized American charity, the Red Cross, in 1881. Her fund raising job focused on overcoming the "I'll-take-care-of-my-family-and-you-take-care-of-yours," independent American image and getting people of all walks of life involved in sharing with others.

By the 1900s the mails were being used to send out appeals for various needs, whereas at first personal contacts and appeals were considered the only means of generating interest.

War relief, of course, brought about a spurt of growth in charitable works by the early 1920s, and later the Great Depression put some who had previously mocked charities in need of help themselves. Franklin Delano Roosevelt, as a victim of polio, prompted much interest in organized health efforts.

Through the period of the thirties and forties, fund raising became a recognized profession, and more and more charitable institutions began turning over the funding work to directors of development, taking that load off the presidents of colleges, chairmen of the boards, and founders of institutions.

New sources of gift money were being explored, such as the deferred gift, which allowed for the insecure prosperity of the post-depression years. By the 1960s many charities were using gift annuities as well as charitable trusts.

My Background in Planned Giving

It was in the 1950s that I left the life insurance business to take a job with a charitable institution.

This institution had been in existence for more than twenty-five years and was reaching millions of people. The work of the institution was paid for by many small gifts, but the organization's interests were expanding and more substantial support was needed.

My job was to try to discover some new gift sources. After studying the field of financial development carefully, I decided the greatest need in fund raising was in the area of *deferred giving*. At that time the management of that institution had in mind encouraging gifts through wills, so this was about all I did at first. Even without special emphasis, they had been receiving a trickling of bequests. Now I was to look for other donors and to see if we could attract other types of deferred gifts. During the four years I was there, we started a gift annuity program and received gifts by way of life estate contracts, revocable living trusts, pooled income plans, and other means.

I have since then chosen to use the term *planned giving* instead of *deferred giving* as a better description of generally the same thing. Not all planned gifts are deferred, of course, but all deferred gifts should be planned. Planned giving includes gifts through wills, trusts, gift annuities, revocable gifts, memorial gifts, life insurance gifts, real estate, and tax gifts.

One of the first priorities in my mind was to find out who we were as an institution. Where did we expect to go with such a planned giving program and would the program *help* people? We took the approach that we could serve people by helping them give their assets at death to our own and other worthy institutions.

Having come out of the field of estate analysis through my life insurance experience, I could see clearly how giving should relate to estate planning. So when a gift to a nonprofit institution resulted from an estate analysis activity, this would become charitable estate planning.

My personal belief is that deferred giving, stewardship work, development work, planned giving (or whatever you choose to call it) is done best by helping the donor look at his entire financial picture before making a substantial gift. I was and still am committed to the belief that if we serve the people and help them give as *they* choose with minimal influence from us, they will experience the joy of freely giving and will not disappoint our institutions in the process. I have found that people cannot resist giving to the institution that provides help in planning their giving.

When I help a person give money or property to the institution of his choice, I serve him in an area of great need in his life. All people seem to have a built-in need to give to someone or some cause. If I just go out to get people's money or property, they sense it. If I help them give, they will sense that too, and when the plans are consummated they will almost always give the largest share to my institution.

In a few short years I saw a good program of planned giving develop. When I left after four years, the organization had an ongoing program that was properly staffed. It has continued to grow in service to the donor while increasing the financial resources of that institution.

What I learned there, which has been confirmed by subsequent efforts for hundreds of other institutions, is this: Components of success in a planned giving program are (1) the validity of the organization, (2) the commitment of the donors, (3) the selection and training of the person to manage the program, and (4) management of the program itself. A failure at any of these points spells trouble in the future of that institution's fund-gathering effort.

Who Are the Planned Givers?

The "market" for planned gifts will probably be no more than three percent of your constituency. A prospect is *more than likely a donor or an ex-donor*. The amount of the gift made currently by a person is not always a good indication of his potential as a planned giver. Some who give a few dollars a year now may make substantial planned gifts later. While people at higher economic levels would be expected to make deferred gifts, we cannot limit our search for the three percent to larger donors only.

Why would *ex-donors* make planned gifts? They may very well be some of our best prospects because they often become "income poor" while remaining "property rich." Many widows, for instance, quit giving because their husbands leave them with all the property they owned—which may have been suitable for them as a couple but is completely wrong for her as a widow. The widow in many instances does not have the husband's income after he is gone. More important, a widow is many times poorly equipped to manage the large sum of money (principal) she received at her husband's death.

The "planned gift market," then, must be searched out. This calls for an ongoing marketing program through the mail, magazine ads and articles, radio/TV, third-party influences, telephone calls, personal visits, banquets, and any other creative mass and individual approaches. To do the best job of marketing such a program, your management needs to seek a highly committed person with strong marketing talents. By committed, I mean a person who has a deep personal interest both in the institution's program and the field of planned giving. He should see his work as being as vital as that of any other person in the institution. (Chapter 4 gives more qualifications for a successful planned giving officer.) Fund gathering or planned giving is the *goal*, but a well-conceived marketing plan is the *technique*.

All institutions, including local churches, small local health agencies, large national institutions, colleges, missions, hospitals, and universities, have a market for planned gifts. It is wise and relatively inexpensive to conduct a market survey for the purpose of obtaining a profile of the persons who give to a particular institution. We have assisted many institutions in obtaining a profile of their various donor classifications. Don't assume that your mission, school, or other institution is like someone else's. (See Chapter 3 for detailed information on how a donor profile works and how it can help you market planned gifts.)

Differences Between Male and Female Givers

In developing a planned giving program, it is important that we understand some basic differences in the way men and women give.

Historically, the man (husband) devotes his life to acquiring; he is generally acquisitive. He spends his life working, earning,

29

accumulating, investing, reinvesting, borrowing, and building his business or profession.

Have you ever wondered why so many men with large earnings tend to give so little to your cause even though they show great interest in so many other ways? The answer—they really feel they can't afford to. High income men have a real problem. They have been called the Poor Little Rich Men of America. The higher their income goes, the more effect the progressive income tax rate has on their net income.

A man 40 to 50 years of age may have two to four children in college; he may support an aged parent; he probably has a cabin on the lake with a boat, a trailer, and a variety of things that cost money. In addition, he probably belongs to one or more business or social clubs. He probably pays large life insurance premiums and year after year finds himself needing to borrow money to pay the balance of his income taxes. Mr. Poor Little Rich Man usually dies seven and a half years before his wife of the same age. Many men marry women two years younger and this leaves their widows with nine-plus years to live alone.

The woman (wife-widow) generally has been observed to be *distributive* by nature. Even though she may be part of the increasing number of working women, she is still the one who "gives" children to the world after which she gives them food and care. She spends and thinks in terms of what money will do immediately to meet needs or provide pleasures. She often manages the income her husband earns. She is constantly giving herself to others. When her husband dies, he will more than likely leave the bulk of the estate to her. She is often in a dilemma because she is faced for the first time with not only the responsibilities she has always had but also the head-of-the-family management responsibilities. She often is not equipped to take over the management of investments.

Soon she recognizes that she does not have her husband's income, and oftentimes his investment objectives are no longer suitable for her present needs. In many cases, she stops or reduces her giving to some or all of the charities they previously had supported together. She may have become "income poor" and "property rich."

If a widow has no heirs to remember as she plans her estate, she may want to consider your institution as her major beneficiary. It is worthwhile to make an effort to help her plan her affairs and to get competent help for her in rearranging her investments to produce more current income for her. As a result of your effort to assist her, you are often able to use a trust instrument or gift annuity to increase her income and make it possible for her to give the remaining trust assets to your institution at her death. Whether a living trust arrangement is indicated or not, she can name your institution as a beneficiary in her will.

Men do make planned giving arrangements. Couples do too. Based on my experience, however, the primary "market" for planned gifts is women over age 50 who have never married or who have been widowed. Planned giving communication for the most part should be directed toward these women.

EXAMPLE: Mrs. Stringer is a widow, age 69. She owns her home worth $68,000 and a cabin at the lake valued at about $18,000. Her husband has left her $70,000 worth of stocks; she owns $15,000 in bonds and has a savings account of $15,000, in addition to her checking account that has an average balance of $2,000. She has several nieces and nephews whom she wishes to remember with $1,000 each through bequests. But she wants the major part of her estate to go to her church, her college, and the local children's hospital. Mrs. Stringer could make these designations in her will.

Or, she could establish a revocable living trust, which would include all of her property. The trust would be managed by a trustee who would pay her the income from the invested assets and provide for her additional needs as they arose. At her death, whatever remains in the trust after her bequests would become gifts in equal shares to the church, the college, and the children's hospital. None of this property would pass through probate and thus more would be available for these interests than if she had included them as bequests in her will. If during her later lifetime she would want to withdraw part or all of her funds, she would have that option without restriction by giving notice. Her plan provides her with peace of mind, help with money management, and the confidence that her estate will benefit causes in which she believes. (It is important that Mrs. Stringer have a will, too, in case she revokes the trust or accumulates assets that are not placed in the trust.)

This case suggests just one way that planned giving can accomplish several good purposes, both for the giver and the institutions he or she supports.

Getting the Orchestra Together

The late Arthur Fiedler directed music of almost any kind. He was "my cup of tea" as far as his taste in music was concerned. I believe his key to selling millions of records and drawing record crowds for decades, in addition to his talent, was his management ability coupled with his sensitivity for his audience. He knew who was to do *what, when, how,* and *why.* He knew for certain who he was and who his audience was, and he, in effect, did target marketing. He had a mission; it was well conceived and managed. He did not plan after getting on stage; he knew what music his people would play and he knew if they were ready to perform. That's what makes success for an orchestra.

A successful planned giving program is like one talented section of a fine orchestra. To be effective, an orchestra must have the stringed instruments, *and* the percussion, *and* the woodwinds, *and* the brass. If one element is overpowering, the music comes out wrong.

As a part of the institution's overall financial development program, there is the planned giving section, the capital campaign section, the volunteer section, and the direct-mail fund raising section; all are related to the job of supporting the institution.

The financial development director carries the responsibility of bringing in the right section to "play" at the right time and with the right balance. A comprehensive financial development program, then, operates with harmony like a great symphony orchestra. And within the planned giving department the planned giving director has his own symphony to put together—balancing the mailings, the phone calls, and the personal visits.

Remember, the conductor is not playing for the ears of the orchestra members; he is playing for the audience. He must know the audience and empathize with his hearers. "Getting to Know You" is a good theme song for the planned giving officer regarding his or her donors. The goal is to "get to know" all about the donors and hope they will "get to know" all about us.

Chapter Three
The Donor Profile

Successful fund raisers *know* their donors and donor prospects—and so do successful planned giving directors. Let me introduce you to the outstanding donor of one nonprofit, religious institution. (We'll call him Mr. Givens.)

The Average Donor

Mr. Givens, age 32, is a professional man who in his student days was served personally by a particular institution. He still keeps in close touch with the local staff people and involves himself in their activities whenever possible. He is primarily interested in this institution's work with students.

Mr. Givens is married and has three children. He lives in a community of about 100,000. His annual income is about $25,000. He does not have a will yet, but, for his income level, he gives generously to six institutions, including this particular one. He reads five or six books a year and reads this institution's magazine thoroughly. He is a church member, a Baptist.

Now the reason Mr. Givens is the outstanding donor of this institution is that he is a composite, a picture of the average donor. When this institution directs a general appeal letter to its donor list, it might as well envision Mr. Givens, his family, his interests, his involvement with the institution, because "Mr. Givens" is the one who will be responding to the appeal.

How do we know?

This institution, for whom I served as a consultant, was able to draw up what we call a "donor profile" from a carefully planned, carefully written donor survey—a four-page questionnaire sent out to a healthy sampling of the donor list. The donor was asked for his help—not his identity—to determine his interests and the institution's effectiveness in communicating its work. The responses were tabulated by the institution's trained staff and then evaluated by an outside professional.

The result was "Mr. Givens." We're not saying that Mr. Givens is the *biggest* donor. He was simply the most representative donor.

Meet the Super Donors

Another personality description fits the *super* donor of this institution, whom we will call Mr. and Mrs. Biggers.

These husband-wife donors are younger than the average donor, contrary to what might be found by many institutions. They are in the 20-to-30-year age bracket. They are generally professional people and thus college graduates. Annual family income is only about a thousand dollars more than the average donor's income. Their main interest is the institution's mission to servicemen, and their secondary interest is in the college campus work.

Normally, when developing mailings on planned giving we would think of approaching the large givers with information on gift annuities, pooled income contracts, and various charitable remainder trusts—because these givers are usually thought to be older. I believe that without a donor survey list we would have made a costly mistake with just such mailings to this organization's super donors—who as I've indicated were in their twenties and thirties.

Instead, we decided to approach these younger donors with an emphasis on gifts of securities followed by a focus on wills. The leads that developed have kept the planned giving officer of this institution very active in contacting qualified donors.

In Contrast . . .

Another institution, however, of the same size mailing list has an average donor of age 60 (one-fourth of the givers are over age 70). The average donor here is a married woman who has been giving to the institution for at least four years. Helping with food production programs overseas is her main concern, and family-planning programs are a secondary interest. She reads as many as twenty-five books a year, has no children at home, and lives in a community of 100,000 to 500,000. Her average income is $18,000 (one-third of the donors are in the over-$28,000 bracket). She does have a will, but it does not include charitable bequests. She owns stocks or corporate bonds, and she contributes to eleven other charitable institutions, including other international relations groups. Her education includes a college degree and some graduate study. She is an active church member, Methodist or Presbyterian.

More Super Donors

As with the first institution, the super donors of this institution are a husband-wife combination. They are over 60, as is the average donor, but they have about *twice* the income.

At about the time of the analysis of this institution's donor profile, the institution was getting ready to do a rather sizeable mailing to introduce the subject of charitable bequests through wills. Because more than three-fourths of the donors indicated they already had wills, this would have been a counterproductive approach.

Instead, because of what was learned from the donor profile study, ideas on how to augment their wills were mailed to these people. For example, it was suggested that they add a codicil that would include the not-for-profit institution as a beneficiary in their wills. They talked about reviewing the will, giving through living trusts, and other ideas that would interest people who have already made a will.

When the profile shows the average donor is over 60, this signals that you have a significant market for life-income type gift arrangements. The experience of this institution bears out the profile. Their donors have been prospects for gift annuities and other types of giving-for-income arrangements.

Increasing numbers of institutions are making surveys and

developing donor profiles to help them do targeted fund raising and, as a result, receive more gifts. A donor profile is something to seriously consider. If you haven't made one, remember your "competition" probably has—your "competition" being all those other colleges, mission societies, denominations, and charitable institutions seeking the same gift dollars you are.

Hit Your Target

Remember the story about the private on the rifle range who shot one hundred rounds and missed the target every time? The sergeant said, "Soldier, where are all those bullets going?"

"I dunno, Sarge," he answered. "All I know is that they're leaving here."

How many planned giving mailings miss because not enough is known about the target? For the following reasons a donor profile should help you make fewer mistakes.

1. It helps you *define* your average donor.
2. It points up the *differences* between the *small, large, super,* and *former* donors.
3. It makes possible the preparation of a *plan of action* based on sound marketing and communication principles.

A donor profile will tell you that what works for another institution may not necessarily work for you. The longer I am in the role of planned giving consultant, the more convinced I become that each institution is unique in terms of its important constituency. An institution is like a person—each one is a priceless original. And it is the little things that often make the difference when it comes to giving. So when starting a program, whether it be direct-mail fund raising or a planned giving program, a market survey that produces a donor profile is invaluable because through it you can get to know your donors.

A donor profile will help you avoid the costly mistake of dropping donors who have stopped giving—just when they may be ready to give you their entire estate.

How Do You Make a Donor Profile?

The profile is the result of a long process that begins with a market survey of donors. (A portion of a typical donor profile survey can be found in Table 1.) After the results are tabulated, reduced to statistics, and carefully analyzed, a profile is prepared. Depending upon the amount of information included in the questionnaire, the profile may be very detailed or somewhat sketchy.

You will need all the tact, diplomacy, and charm you can muster to construct a questionnaire that will not displease your donors and still yield the information you need.

Don't try to rush it. Plan to spend at least two weeks developing your questionnaire and accompanying letter. Take your time writing it . . . and take time to get it approved by all your colleagues. Expect to see it go through several drafts before everyone agrees on it. Get outside assistance. Here's one place the professional can give invaluable help.

The information you should seek on a donor survey really depends upon what you want to accomplish. First, you *don't* want to make the survey so long that only a few will take the time to complete and return it. But second, neither do you want to make it so short it doesn't include enough meaningful information to make the project worthwhile.

After a series of tests, Mr. Ralph Sanders, the best professional I know for designing donor profiles, says,

> I've personally concluded that a four-page questionnaire in large type with lots of white space is the right length. Even four pages is long, but it really takes that much space to accommodate the questions. And in timing tests, I've found that the four-page surveys I've done can be completed by the average person in five minutes—the shortest time was three minutes and the longest time was ten.[1]

---

[1]Ralph Sanders is executive vice-president of World Neighbors, Inc. Many of the ideas in this section are drawn from Mr. Sanders's lectures at seminars of the National Planned Giving Institute, sponsored by Robert F. Sharpe & Co., Inc., and are used by permission.

TABLE 1
SAMPLE FIRST PAGE OF DONOR PROFILE SURVEY

SURVEY OF FRIENDS OF (Name of institution)

INSTRUCTIONS: This is an anonymous survey—there's no need to sign your name. Please answer the questions frankly. If a question doesn't apply, leave it blank and move on to the next question. Make an "X" or check mark in the blank in front of the answer which applies best. If there are questions you would prefer not to answer, skip them. Should you care to comment at greater length than is possible in the survey, feel free to enclose such thoughts on a separate sheet. After completing the survey, please return it as soon as possible in the postage-paid reply envelope provided.

1. Which member of your family is most interested in (name of institution)
   _____man
   _____woman
   _____both husband and wife

2. What is your age?
   _____under 25   _____51 to 64
   _____26 to 35   _____65 and over
   _____36 to 50

3. What is your marital status?
   _____married   _____widowed
   _____single   _____divorced

4. How long have you been a contributor to (name of institution)
   _____less than a year   _____four to nine years
   _____one to three years   _____over ten years

5. How did you first learn of (name of institution)? Check only one:
   _____through a friend
   _____through a printed brochure
   _____through a tour or personal visit
   _____through a speaker
   _____through school or church
   _____through a newspaper article
   _____through radio or television
   _____through a special event
   _____I personally was helped by _____
   _____other (please specify):_____

This is the information you should try to obtain:

1. Sex
2. Age

3. Marital status

4. Length of time they've been contributing to the program

5. How they learned of the program

6. What interests them most about the program

7. How many books and magazines they read last year

8. How carefully they read our materials—letters, newsletters, reports

9. Number and ages of children

10. Size of their community

11. Amount of annual family income

12. Whether or not they have a will

13. If so, whether or not it includes charitable bequests

14. Whether or not they own a gift annuity

15. Whether or not they own stocks or bonds or mutual funds

16. Their educational goals or accomplishments

17. Church preference

18. Whether or not they are church members

19. Civic clubs to which they belong

20. Their other charitable interests

(Some of these questions might have little application for your institution, and you might have other questions that apply in your situation only.)

What You Will Discover

There's one other question I would always include on my questionnaire—and it just might be the most important of all. It is simply this: "Is there a job that we are not presently doing that you think we should do?" Then provide writing space. You will learn a great deal. Some of the answers you get in the form of constructive criticism are most valuable. Through the survey, for example—

• You may find that many of your donors read a magazine in which you once considered advertising, but didn't. Now you may want to reconsider.

- You may find that you have many low-income donors who own real estate. This is a signal for you to suggest they raise their incomes by trading real estate for retained income plans.

- You will find out things they like about you that you never suspected, and you can stress this feature to win more friends. You will also find out what they *don't* like, and perhaps you can make changes that will help.

- You will find out where to locate new donors. If your institution appeals to middle-aged married women in small towns, you can save money on future mailings by targeting on small towns.

- You will gain valuable information for planning your general fund raising program.

A Typical Discovery

Here's what one profile might sound like for a small church-related liberal arts college.

The average donor to a small private college is a married woman about forty-five years of age who has been contributing for about five years. Her interests at the college are first, campus development, and second, financial aid to needy students. She reads about six books a year and subscribes to three magazines. She receives both the bimonthly college newsletters and the quarterly president's letters. She reads the newsletters "thoroughly" and "skims" the president's letters.

She has three children, one of whom is still at home. She lives in a community of about 50,000. Annual family income is $18,000. She may have a will, but it doesn't include charitable bequests. She has little stock. Last year she contributed to eight charitable institutions including possibly one other small college. She prefers to give cash once or twice a year. She attended at least three years of college—quite likely this one—and probably completed a bachelor's degree. She is a church member, most likely a Presbyterian.

Now suppose you were this college's president or development officer. Wouldn't a profile like this help you greatly in determining the best course of action for planning your general fund raising and deferred giving programs? The profile I just gave was only the general, "average" donor profile. Separate profiles can be prepared also for small donors, large donors, super donors, former donors, and other special groups.

Some Words of Caution

Don't try to do it all yourself. Professional help is available and you should use it as much as possible. If you can't afford to have an outside firm do the entire job, at least bring one in for the two most important phases—(1) preparing your questionnaire and (2) making your final analysis. You need the outside professional view. Even the best of us will bend those figures somewhat to fit our preconceived notions. A donor profile will give you confidence as you approach your present donors and will give you a clear picture of the kind of person most likely to become a new donor.

What to Do with the Completed Survey

Test it. If the returns suggest that your donors own several stocks, plan a mailing on giving stocks. If it pulls better than average, your survey must have been right. If it doesn't, your survey may have been off base on that point. Remember, you have surveyed only *some* of your donors, a sample. You hope it was a typical sample, but only testing will tell.

For example, one institution included the question, "Would you rather pay the postage or have us pay it when you send your gift?" Nearly 80 percent said they would rather pay the postage.

Based on this finding alone, I don't believe this institution should even consider not sending their postage-paid business reply envelopes. Such a decision would almost certainly cost the institution gift dollars. This kind of question has a high "Yes" bias, because who wants to indicate they have neither the funds nor the inclination to furnish a postage stamp? Since most donors give impulsively and most prospective donors (even

TABLE 2
SAMPLE SURVEY COVER LETTER

(Date)

Dear Friend:

Your contributions to XYZ have been a welcome source of help to us—and now we need another kind of assistance to help us strengthen and improve our program.

For that reason, I am enclosing a "Survey of Friends of XYZ." And I will certainly appreciate it if you will answer the questions and return the survey at your earliest possible convenience. Your response will give us the needed data to enable us to:

1. Reflect faithfully the wishes and intentions of our donors;
2. Let our overseas associates know the character of those who make the program possible;
3. Expand our base of support . . . without wasting efforts or funds; and
4. Gain insights which we may have overlooked.

Let me stress that this is an anonymous survey. You need not sign your name. And the reply envelope which is enclosed has no coding—it doesn't even need a stamp! Some of the questions may seem rather personal, but they really will help us to understand better our people and our task. However, if there's any part of the survey you'd prefer not to answer, just skip that portion—leave it blank—and move on to the next part.

Since this survey is anonymous, I won't have a chance to thank you for helping us, so let me thank you now. Your answers will assist us greatly as we seek to do an ever-improving job in the future. Warm and good wishes.

Sincerely yours,

those saying they will pay the postage) probably will not have a stamp handy, they will tend to delay action and never send the gift. The only way to be certain is to test, test, test.

Apply it. How do you apply the results from your completed donor profile? First, consider the type of information the survey brought you. You may find out that most of your donors heard about you in a denominational magazine and very few are receiving or reading your newsletter—a sign that you should perhaps beef up the former and give up the latter.

You may learn that many donors want you to do something you're already doing only they don't *know* it. So you need to tell them about it again, this time more emphatically.

You may discover that a large majority of your donors are much older than you thought, which gives you two signals: (1) You need to plan effective ways of adding new names to the mailing list, and (2) a planned giving appeal to the present mailing list is definitely appropriate. Many could be ready for will-making or for substantial income giving.

An institution I am acquainted with did a donor survey by breaking down individual contributors into small, large, and super donors and then decided how many names from each group would be surveyed. To get a good random geographical sample, they arranged to select every third, fifth, or tenth name, depending upon the category.

To get the surveys to the donors, they prepared a special mailing package consisting of the following items:

1. A cover letter from the president. The letter (see a sample of this type of letter in Table 2) explained the need for the survey and asked for their help.
2. A four-page questionnaire.
3. A number 9 business reply envelope (postage-paid).

To emphasize further the anonymous feature, the mailing was sent at the nonprofit bulk rate and the letter was of the printed "Dear Friend" variety. The institution had no way of knowing what the response would be. Knowledgeable executives from several other institutions felt that anywhere from a 15 to 25 percent donor response would be a smashing success. This institution was delighted to receive a 40 percent response. And a few donors even insisted on sending along a contribution with their "anonymous" questionnaire!

It is important to stress both in the letter and on the questionnaire that if there are questions the donor prefers *not* to answer, he should just skip that section and move on to the next. You may be surprised, however, to find how few people skip any questions. Interestingly enough, the people who often skip the annual income section are not the large and super donors—but some of the small donors. Most people making sizeable incomes seem proud of the fact.

Many donors will not want to fill out the questionnaire. They should know they are free to toss it aside (as obviously many do) and simply ignore it.

Additional Tips on Donor Surveys

Ralph Sanders, who as I indicated earlier has helped numerous institutions plan and evaluate their donor surveys, offers the following tips to those who are serious about knowing their donors through a donor profile:

1. *Be sure management is behind the donor survey*. Your survey may turn up some pretty surprising information about your donors and what they think about you. There may be areas you need to change before you can attract new donors. If your management is too rigid to change "regardless," don't waste time with the survey.

2. *Find a competent person to help you*. Planning, mailing, tabulating, and coordinating a survey involves endless details. Your time is simply too valuable to get deeply involved in the mechanics. Find a reliable person with an eye for fine detail and put this person in charge of the project. I hired a part-time helper who had experience in accounting and secretarial work for our survey, and it kept her busy half days for six months. In fact, our survey, which was an extremely large one, involved over six hundred working hours.

3. *Work out mailing details far in advance*. Many groups will have to separate manually their donor groups (small, large, super, former), and this takes time. Sometimes several months of advance work are needed before the envelopes are addressed and sorted. This should be done well before the survey is ready to mail.

4. *Questionnaire coding.* Be sure the different question-naires to the different donor groups are coded differently, so that if they are returned in a different envelope from the one you sent, they still can be tabulated in the proper category. Make certain you can identify small, large, and super donors—and keep each group separate. A good method is simply to print the questionnaires on different colored stock.

5. *Read the most interesting questionnaires yourself.* Set up a system for all of the surveys with interesting comments to be routed to your desk. In fact, it would be worthwhile to skim through all of them just to get a better idea of the total picture. (For months one time, I took home twenty-five each night and one hundred on weekends.) Plan to review all of the super and large donor questionnaires yourself, for in reading through each one you get a better feel for the people.

6. *Keep up with the tabulating.* As soon as the returns start coming in, get a team started on tabulating the results. Don't wait until all the surveys are in to begin. And it's better if only a couple of people—the same ones—do the tabulating and coding so each questionnaire rating is consistent. The people you choose should be dependable, and this is definitely not the place to use part-time help. The fewer people tabulating the better. A few errors in tabulating will throw your results off badly and cause serious mistakes in the final analysis.

7. *Survey a large sample of your donors.* Try to include as many people of each donor group in your survey as your budget will allow. If you have ten thousand donors, but you can only mail questionnaires to 10 percent of these, your result may not be meaningful at all. Remember, of the one thousand you mail, perhaps only three hundred will respond. And to base your entire program on what 3 percent of your donors say is an excellent example of putting all your eggs in one basket. For safety's sake, I would urge you to survey enough donors so that your total response would be at least 10 percent of your constituency. And to get a 10 percent response you will need to mail to between 30 to 40 percent of your donors.

8. *Prepare the analysis and donor profile with great care.* The analysis of the survey is the heart of it. Should it be done poorly, it would be worse than no profile at all. Don't rush into drafting the analysis of what all your figures mean. If possible, get some professional help. Then, after you have prepared the analysis, with statistics in hand go over it again and again asking yourself: "Is this really what these figures mean?"

9. *Test the results before accepting them without qualification.* Before staking your entire program on the survey, especially if you've done all the work yourself, test some of the results. Perhaps you have asked your donors to rank their top interests in your program as one, two, or three. Build several appeal letters around the top interests, remembering that what was the top interest for the super donors may not even make the list of the small donors. Then compare the gift response to those letters with that of previous letters. Was it better? While your profile was prepared under sound, scientific market-research principles, it can be fallible simply because you have only received the opinions of *some* of your donors. It is always possible that on a particular question or two, the 5 or 7 or 12 percent who responded to your survey really weren't typical. This is unlikely, perhaps, but always possible.

Summary

A donor profile offers your institution a number of advantages. It will give you insights into your donors, the type of people they are, where they come from, what they like and don't like about you, and even how they read your publications. When you get that information, *use it*—not only to do a better job in communicating with them and in fund raising but also to help improve your institution's programs in any areas where the donors have made good suggestions. The donor profile gives you the basic information you need. Your task is to translate that information into new service *to* and dollars *from* your constituent donors.

Chapter Four
The Successful Planned
Giving Officer

In my opinion, there are *six important* conditions that a planned giving officer must maintain to be successful.

A Personal Interest in the Organization

Would you be interested in your institution even if you didn't work for it? Would you give it your own money?

If the smell of antiseptic makes you feel faint, you may not belong in the development department of a hospital. You could have an outside entrance to your office and arrange to meet the hospital staff on the parking lot, but getting to know the patients and developing a conversational knowledge of the facilities would be difficult.

If you enjoy children only when they are sleeping or on someone else's lap, you aren't the most likely candidate to write an appeal letter with a warm beginning like, "Would you like to know how to hug one hundred thousand kids. . . ."

If you found college to be the most trying four years (or five or six years!) of your life, regardless of how grateful you are for your education, you are not likely to have a knack for attracting students or funds for a university.

In other words, you need to have a personal interest in the work of the institution you are promoting. If you don't, your lack of interest can come across in everything you do (or don't do).

Empathy for Those Who Support the Organization

It helps, too, if you have empathy for your donors and donor prospects. Fred Alexander says empathy is that inborn capacity to *feel* with the other person, to look at things from his or her viewpoint.[1] Some say this is a nontransferable quality.

Many qualified observers, for example, believe that too much emphasis is placed on scientific aptitudes in the selection and qualifying of medical students. More weight should be given to those factors in human personality that are responsive and sympathetic to the needs of people.

Somewhat the same thing may be said of the criteria for planned giving officers. The field does not really need people who are adept at "figures," who know all about law and taxation. The need is for men and women who basically love and understand people.

The Ability to Maintain the Objective

A professional planned giving officer concentrates his efforts on seeing people and promoting the work of the institution. A well-trained office staff can take care of such details as getting out mailings, following up on routine inquiries, qualifying prospects, and handling the paper work. This is not to say you shouldn't keep up with what's happening at the office. But once you have your program well established, a competent staff will be able to keep it in motion, making certain decisions on their own. Your office responsibilities are to be strictly administrative and creative.

The same principle applies to the planned giving program. Learn the concepts of planned giving and know all the different ways a person can support your institution. Every competent planned giving officer should know how the various plans

---

[1]These ideas are suggested by Fred Alexander, institutional development consultant with over twenty-five years of experience in financial development management. Much of this material was prepared and presented for the National Planned Giving Institute, sponsored by Robert F. Sharpe & Co., Inc.

work, the advantages of each, and the tax implications. (See Chapter 17 on taxes.)

This does not mean you have to know every treasury regulation, revenue ruling, or court decision that is handed down. In fact, unless you are actively engaged in legal work in a professional manner on a daily basis, I suggest this is an impossibility.

How much do you need to know? You need to know enough to go into a home or office, interview a prospect, obtain the right information, and recognize planned giving potential.

For example, finding out that Mrs. Jones, age 75, has the desire and the financial ability to support your institution and needs some type of income for life should tell you that she is a candidate for a gift annuity, revocable living trust, or charitable remainder trust.

The point is, don't spend so much of your time trying to learn everything that you find yourself tied to a desk day in and day out with no time to make calls. This is defeating the purpose. It is usually less expensive to pay $150 an hour to someone who specializes in taxation than it is to take time to become an expert yourself.

Maintain the objective—see people today.

The Right Amount of Aggressiveness

We are not saying planned giving officers cannot be fired-up, aggressive, super salespeople. They have to be personable, of course, and persuasive. They should like people and leave a good impression.

Yet, *they are not people who come on strong*. You should refrain from being the dynamic one to be remembered out of a group of twelve.

Planned giving people are not showmen. They don't play to an audience in an overt way. As a matter of fact, they have the capacity, if they are really good, to play themselves down and take a back seat. What we normally think of as salesman-like qualities can sometimes be a handicap. For example, during the ten years that I was in the insurance business, I was constantly searching out and learning better sales techniques. When I became involved in the planned giving field, I found I had to "unlearn" some of these techniques. I learned that instead of trying to get my foot in the door so I could get inside and start talking, I had to back in the door, in a sense, and learn to sit down and *listen*. When I learned how to "hear between the lines," the achievement was phenomenal!

A person who has been in the limelight or is highly self-expressive is most likely a poor choice for a planned giving officer.

Thorough Understanding of the Job Description

If you don't know where you are going, it is almost impossible to get there. Lack of a *clear* job description is one of the major reasons for failure on the part of planned giving officers for not-for-profit institutions. Basic areas of responsibility should be well-defined before you take the job, and in addition there should be guidelines as to how you will spend your time and carry out the program.

Already existing plans, which governed your predecessor's responsibilities, are relatively easy to modify. In other words, the planned giving officer should not feel locked in by a possibly outdated description of his job. It will help if the board will listen to and answer your questions about the job description *before* appointing you to the office.

Find out if you are being hired to "hold the hands" of an already loyal and committed planned gifts constituency, or if you are expected to start right out from scratch and actually determine who the qualified constituents are. Is there a planned gifts committee or field representatives with whom you will work, or will you help form a board of volunteer workers and policy makers?

If you are hiring a planned giving officer, understand that salary considerations are important to the job description. If the salary is too low, the person becomes a sitting duck for other offers. If the salary is too high, problems are created within your institution. A safe figure would be a salary equivalent to other second or third level managers whose training and successful experience are already proven. I suggest a salary not greater than 80 percent of the chief executive's salary. Certainly there should be a full schedule of benefits to complement the salary.

Occasionally, concessions will have to be made to allow an especially competent man to function to some extent outside the institution. He may lecture, consult, or write. If he is talented, he should be allowed reasonable latitude.

No commissions, please! A planned giving officer should never be put under the pressure of measuring his effectiveness by the number of giving contracts he is able to complete. Whether he feels it or not, working on a commission basis will hinder his ability to serve the donor's and the institution's best interests. I feel strongly about this, having seen the unhappy results in more than one institution where the field men operated on a commission basis.

The Need for Latitude and Authority

It is essential that a planned giving officer know what is expected of him when he takes the job. The planned giving program should be the institution's program, *not* the planned giving officer's program. However, each man or woman coming to the job must have the latitude and freedom to design, have approved, and carry out new ideas for the program.

Be sure you have access to your supervisor with freedom also to interact personally with members of the board. And once your plans are made and approved, you must have the authority to carry them out. But remember: With authority comes responsibility and accountability.

In one situation a competent planned gifts director was brought aboard but soon discovered himself straining under the empire-building arm of the comptroller who was unwilling to go along with policies initiated in the planned giving office. The comptroller, who had the responsibility of *allocating* funds, was exercising a self-appointed prerogative to assist in the *procuring* of funds. In the tricky area of planned giving, such a situation may end in disaster for the comptroller, the planned giving officer, and the institution itself.

Do You Approximate This Character Profile?

We talked earlier about the profile of an average donor to your institution. Let's take a look in the other direction and see what the composite, successful planned giving officer is like.

- He is a college graduate.
- He already knows or has the aptitude to learn the ropes of personal estate planning.
- He has executive ability.
- He is a team worker, not a "loner."
- The planned giving officer has an understanding of systems management and some practical skills related to that field.
- He is adept at communicating with people, and he is personally appealing in one-to-one situations.
- He *must* be sympathetic to the cause he espouses.

In a study by Worthington, Hurst, and Associates of Chicago,[2] psychological consultants to industry, some interesting observations about development officers were uncovered. We believe these characteristics apply to planned gifts officers as well:

- Most development people come from modest backgrounds but have taken the opportunity to rise significantly above the social status of their fathers. Rarely, we are told by sociologists, does a person rise more than one level of social class within his generation. Characteristically, development officers have exemplified a life-style that rises above the circumstances and backgrounds of their pasts.

[2]Theodore Hurst is president of Worthington, Hurst, and Associates. His study was conducted in 1960 at the direction of the American College Public Relations Association, which designated twenty-one men as representative of successful development officers of colleges and universities for the research project.

53

- Development officers often come from families where the number of children is greater than the average per family for the population at large. It was noted, however, that there was no clear pattern as to placement, age-wise, within the family.
- All of the people sampled in this particular study had achieved their bachelor's degree. It would thus appear that the baccalaureate degree is the minimum educational requisite for the development officer.

Other favorable personal characteristics revealed in this study include:

- A liberal arts background. Beware of the man whose record indicates a history of "snap" courses.
- A history of participation in a wide variety of extracurricular activities in high school and college. Athletics, the school paper or yearbook, drama, speech, etc., are all good indicators.
- A standing in the upper 10 percent of the class in high school and college. A person beneath the upper 25 percent would be a statistical risk.
- A background of high school and college class or social offices and the attainment of scholastic and social honors.
- Evidence, usually indicated by one's age at college graduation, that the person can complete his work on schedule. The person who did not receive his degree until his late twenties or thirties, unless this delay was caused by illness or military service, usually has less chance of succeeding in this field.

Indicators show that a person who is single or divorced and over 35 will *generally* be a weak selection but, of course, there are exceptions. The successful officer will take traveling as a necessity, but not necessarily as something that he looks forward to, especially if traveling takes up more than 25 or 30 percent of his time. In some cases development officers can travel as much as 50 to 70 percent of their time, but in terms of their own family relationships, this should be discouraged.

Beware of the heavy drinker or smoker and the person who is seriously overweight. Your donors' first impressions are important.

Generally the successful planned giving officer has the ability to *wait for results*, deferring his own rewards. Obviously, this person has to be someone who has faith in what he is doing and the processes he goes through, knowing that ultimately his work will bear fruit. He often cannot see the daily results of his efforts. This may also mean that the person needs the kinds of personal relationships that can encourage and support him during times of potential discouragement. It is very difficult for most people to work for months or years before they can be certain that what they have done has been effective.

Naturally, as with any list of positive or negative attributes, almost every successful man or woman will show exceptions to the items listed. The emphasis here is not necessarily on individual personal characteristics, but rather personality patterns. A man or woman who has many of the positive attributes and few of the negative ones will have a good chance of success.

Chapter Five
Launching a Planned
Giving Program

Now that we've discussed why a planned giving program can be effective and how to select a qualified planned giving officer, it's time to get the program underway.

Choosing Your Committee

One immediate help in getting started with a planned gifts program is to recruit a committee of about five people who know as many of the institution's constituents as possible. These could be officers of the institution, friends, or volunteers.

This committee can list the top current donors known to them. Many of these donors are immediate prospects for planned gifts. The larger list of donors and nondonors will have to be approached through direct mail or other methods so that planned giving prospects can be discovered.

Crass as it may sound, some of the prospects discovered through these methods will evidently be "critical." Due to illness or old age, they should be approached immediately. These will be the first visits of the planned giving officer. Perhaps the president of the institution should initiate the visit or participate in it. There is little need to have an extensive background in planned giving in order to make this type of simple cultivation visit and possibly ask the donor to consider including the institution in his or her will.

Every member of the institution ought to act as a "bird dog" or prospect-finder for the officer in charge of planned gifts.

Choosing a Secretary

The successful planned giving secretary will be a mature person with good office skills and an excellent record in getting along with people. The planned giving officer himself should choose this secretary with whom he will have to work closely. The offices for the planned giving department should be close to the other administrative offices, and there should be at least two rooms—one for the secretary and a private office for the planned giving director.

Continuing Education

A first-rate planned giving officer will outline for himself a continuing study program to keep abreast of developments in this field. Training seminars, cassette studies, magazines, and books on related subjects need to be included in his budget and time schedules. Subscriptions to periodicals directed to financial development officers are a wise use of money.

It is vitally important that the new planned giving officer establish early in his career the habit of constant study of the planned gifts field. Changes in tax laws make it expedient to keep updated constantly in order to be able to consult with his donor-clients and with other experienced professionals in the field. However, again I emphasize that he does not need to be a tax expert. He must also learn to conduct thorough research on all of the prospects that he or others may develop.

Unfortunately, there are not many formal learning opportunities available for those in the planned gift field. We have therefore chosen to incorporate such material into the National Planned Giving Institute. However, in addition to our own training program, we recommend several other seminars. Another important way to learn about planned giving is to attend some of the national conferences sponsored by the Committee on Gift Annuities, the Christian Stewardship Council, the National Catholic Development Conference, and the National Council of Churches.

To keep up to date, the planned giving officer should take the opportunity to complete a pertinent course or two at night school. He could take courses that deal with trusts, wills, life insurance, and accounting. These will help him get a basic understanding of the subject material. The well-informed people in this field observe a regular study period. One successful planned giving officer studied thirty hours a month for the first year and continued to study this field fifteen to twenty hours a month for several years.

One informal but very helpful way a planned giving officer can learn is to seek regular meetings with an attorney, a trust officer of a bank, a life underwriter, a certified public accountant (CPA), and an investment broker. Taking these professional people to lunch will help the planned giving officer learn as much as he can about their professions.

Finally, he should make personal calls as soon as possible after getting into planned giving. This is the best training of all. The three most valuable words in the English language for any person dealing in this highly technical and complicated field are "I don't know," and the sentence should continue, "but I can find out and I will get an answer for you as soon as possible."

In the process of learning, there are a few things the planned giving officer doesn't want to learn:

1. Don't learn how to push a prospect into a corner and get him to sign on the dotted line. (The National Planned Giving Institute does not offer a seminar on "How to Close." The able planned giving officer knows he begins closing an arrangement as soon as discussion of the arrangement with the prospect begins.)

2. Don't become a tax expert and try to use tax deductions as the prime motivator for giving. It has been said, "When a person who is properly motivated gives, he enjoys it and it costs him nothing because giving is a benefit. But when he gives solely to get tax deductions, it will always cost him the part of his gift he cannot deduct."

3. *Remember,* when the planned giving officer goes out to see people, if his goal is only to get their money, they will sense it and do little for the institution. But if he goes out with the goal in mind to help the person give to the institution of

his choice, he will serve the prospect and reap great financial reward for your institution.

The Title

Titles can help. They suggest authority, representation, a position of trust, and ability. Planned giving officers may answer to the title of—

Vice-President for Planned Giving
Director of Planned Giving
Assistant to the President for Planned Giving
Planned Giving Consultant
Director of Estates, Wills, and Trusts

Many of an institution's constituents believe they are important enough to be called on by the president himself. Therefore, the planned giving representative needs a prestigious title. He should be introduced to the donors through an article and photo in the house publication, a release to the local newspaper and television stations, and perhaps a small brochure or a letter from the president.

Using Professional Counsel

If a professional consultant is on the job when the planned giving officer arrives, the consultant can help in getting the department and the director functioning and productive with greater speed than could otherwise be achieved.

One of the hazards of deferred gifts cultivation lies in the fact that the activities of the department in some areas are long-range, and hence, apparently *do not have to be immediately productive. But there is necessity for production just as soon as possible.* The department should not be a dead weight on the institution any longer than necessary. There are moves to make that will help the new planned giving person and the department become productive more quickly.

The consultant can act as a motivator to the new officer. He can provide orientation and direction as the officer moves out into the field. This will break the chain that invariably begins to tie planned giving directors to their desks, eliminating their function in the field.

The consultant, then, provides the quick start necessary to the planned giving department. This will make the department productive much more quickly and will help the new person avoid the feeling that he is not actually earning his salary. The consultant's experience and guidance is invaluable at this point.

How All This Can Work

Mr. John West, we will call him, works for the National Not-for-Profit Institution. He is 33 years old and came into his planned giving position from the general contracting business.

During his first year in the planned giving officer's role, he became an excellent student. He completed a four-week planned giving school that consisted of 112 hours of seminar, institute, and workshop experiences. John came to the school one week out of each three months, then returned to his headquarters where he worked hard to get his program moving.

John's first step was to get acquainted with the people with whom he would be working and to establish guidelines for his job. An office was provided and a qualified secretary was employed.

After a study of the various in-house mailing lists, he helped set up an internal filing system. Then he carefully reviewed what had already been done in planned giving by his organization over the years. Policy was established for handling planned giving contracts, reporting to donors, and making payments and investments.

John realized that the best results for the donor and the institution could be obtained by working on an estate analysis basis. This meant not only learning to use the various planned giving contracts and trusts, and the basic tax considerations, but also learning how these methods of giving would become tools of charitable estate planning.

He soon found out that he did not have to be either a tax expert or a lawyer. He hired competent legal counsel to advise him. Counsel for the institution reviewed its constitution and bylaws and determined legal requirements for operating in the various states.

There was a general concern on the part of management that they did not really know their donors. A market survey was completed, which resulted in a profile of their various classifications of donors. From this profile John learned the general make-up of the institution's present donors.

Now that he had an internal system under good management and knew his donors' gifts would be prudently invested, John could start an advertising and promotion program.

The vehicle he had for reaching the donors who resided in every state in the union was a bimonthly magazine reaching out to more than one hundred thousand people. About thirty thousand were donors; the others were former donors or new names added over the years.

Some of the questions John had were, "Who should we try to reach for planned gifts? And how? Will the management and board have the patience to wait while paying for this program?" Fortunately, Mr. West had strong backing from management.

First, articles on wills, revocable trusts, and gift annuities were placed in their bimonthly magazine. This was an inexpensive way to reach everybody on the list using a low-key informational approach. (These articles were written with John West's by-line to introduce him and build confidence in him.)

Second, a series of four direct mailings to donors and to a portion of the former donors was planned for the first year. The mailing package included a letter from the president, a brochure with a response device, and a number 9 business reply envelope. The first two mailings were about wills, the third about revocable living trusts, and the last about gift annuities. Responses began to come in by the hundreds from all over America.

Good planning was completed before the promotion program started so when responses came in, his staff was prepared to answer them immediately.

The plan consisted of answering questions related to the subject in a letter and the sending of the booklet offered. In thirty days a second letter and booklet were sent. In another thirty days a third letter and a booklet were sent and the prospect was encouraged to take action.

Realizing that you can do just so much by mail, John's plan included a careful analysis of each inquiry, looking for comments made by the prospect. At any point when it seemed appropriate, he would deviate from his plan and telephone the person to arrange a visit.

Soon after the mailing and article program began, he was traveling throughout the country to see his best prospects. One recent week he spent 26 hours in the air, drove a rental car 1,300 miles, and had 15 face-to-face interviews resulting in planned gifts totaling $600,000.

John has completed unitrusts, annuity trusts, revocable living trusts, gift annuities, bequests, contracts for land, and large current gifts.

This program is less than four years old and to date planned giving arrangements are well over $3 million. John fully expects the total to reach the $5 million mark by the end of the fiscal year. These totals, of course, do not include expected bequests.

John has now begun a memorial gifts program in order to secure more prospects for planned giving and also to help pay the current cost of his planned giving program.

He is traveling more than 50 percent of his time and is seeing or telephoning people almost daily. He has never been able to contact personally all the people who have indicated an interest. He has already added another person to the planned giving staff.

Three Ingredients of Success

For a successful planned giving program any institution needs:

1. A planned giving officer with empathy who can and will learn, initiate, and work. Three words should be indelibly printed on a planned giving officer's mind—*research, judgment, work*.

2. A purpose that is worthy of their donors' support, a proven history of giving donors a good "return" on their gifts, and a strong support base.

3. A management that can plan a program prudently, fund it adequately, and wait for results.

Chapter Six
The Three Functions: Planning, Developing, and Managing

If an institution hesitates to launch a planned giving program, it is probably because the board of trustees believes results from planned giving are too far in the future and too indefinite to justify the time and money needed to start the program. Board members sometimes fail to get beyond these fears.

Here is motivation for the board of trustees: Documented experiences of institutions who have established histories in the field of planned giving and those that are just beginning show that productive income is often available *within* three years.

Planned giving can add a new dimension to almost every development program and may produce "now" income in a short time. The keys to an effective planned giving program are (1) proper planning, (2) consistent developing and marketing, and (3) prudent managing.

Proper Planning

When starting a planned giving program, careful planning is the first step. Planning (or lack thereof) is *always* paid for. If you *don't* plan, the cost can be great because of the lost gift income. It has been said that the cost can be tens of thousands, hundreds of thousands, or even millions of dollars; and eventually you do the planning, if you are to have a viable planned giving program.

Can you name your top ten donors? How much gift income comes to your institution from the top ten sources—the top 110 sources? And how much from all the rest?

I believe the goal of most charitable institutions should be to receive one-third from the top ten sources, one-third from the next one hundred sources, and the other one-third from all the other sources on the list regardless of the number. I am sure you can argue, "Our institution is *different,* because we have a massive number of donors who give small amounts and we prefer not to become dependent on a few large gifts."

What I am proposing is that you continue building your small donor group by increasing its number and securing as many small gifts as possible. However, if I were the chief executive officer, I would set a goal for my development department that in five years I could have one-third of our gift income coming from ten sources, one-third from one hundred sources, and one-third from all the rest.

Impossible? Let me define a "source." A source is any donor: a foundation or corporation, an individual, a matured bequest, a matured charitable remainder interest of a trust, etc. (Incidentally, you should become an expert on larger donors, perhaps the top 110 plus another 110 of your best prospective givers. These people and institutions should be contacted personally by the chief executive officer, the planned giving officer [or a representative of that office], or carefully selected, effective volunteers. Careful judgment backed up by adequate research is essential. Keep this group out of the "crowd" of donors and cultivate them with great care.)

Here is how your income—your sources—might come in. Let's suppose your institution's annual gift income is $1,500,000.

Donor A dies and leaves	$250,000 in his will
Donor B dies and leaves	50,000 in trust
Foundation C gives	50,000 cash
Corporation D gives	40,000 cash
Donors E and F give	
$25,000 each	50,000 cash

Foundation G gives	20,000 cash
Corporation H gives	15,000 cash
Donor I gives	15,000 cash
Donor J gives	10,000 cash

This totals $500,000. The next 100 top donors give another $500,000 in gifts ranging from $3,000 to $10,000 from all kinds of sources. The other $500,000 would come from 80,000 small donors.

I realize this may seem idealistic, but a growing number of institutions are convinced this plan works. *It doesn't just happen.* The board, chief executive officer, planned giving officer, and all others in top management work to this end. They *make it* happen.

There are cases, of course, where one gift might exceed the annual budget. I assure you this is the exception and not the general rule. For example, one of our clients has an annual gift budget of $486,000. During one year they received a percentage of the residue of a deceased donor's will totaling $510,000.

A strong effort should be made constantly by the organization's management in all areas of fund gathering. If this is to happen in your institution five years from now, careful planning and a concentrated development effort has to be made today. A goal must be set.

How did I come to this conclusion?

Look at the life insurance business. What percentage of a salesman's earnings are from the top ten buyers? For many agents, one-fourth, one-third, or one-half of their income comes from these top ten clients. In real estate, how important are the ten largest real estate buyers each year? The salesman's income is affected by these buyers in much the same way as those of the life insurance agent. In one church of three hundred members, half of the income is provided by the top sixteen givers.

Our own business bears out this same success pattern: 29 percent of our business in a recent year came from the top 10 customer-clients, and the next 100 institutions provided 42 percent, which means that 71 percent of our business came from the top 110 institutions we serve. The 29 percent balance came from about 2,000 other institutions.

The "10-110-all-the-rest" idea was not originally mine. I heard it years ago and have lived with it and watched it long enough to see a consistent pattern for success. Haven't you heard that 15 percent of the salesmen make 85 percent of the commissions? This is the same basic statistic. Understanding this basic pattern and keeping it in view as you plan could well be the most important concept you learn in this book.

The top 110 donors will become your best prospects for planned giving cultivation. These donors can also become effective people in helping you find others like them. These large gifts are so vital to your future that every effort needs to be made to secure bequests, trusts, gift annuities, or other planned gifts that will in effect endow the giver's annual gifts for a few years after death or in perpetuity. These kinds of gifts do not usually come in unless they are worked for by a carefully equipped planned giving officer who has a properly planned program for handling such gifts.

The Planning Function

The *planning* function is primarily a board of trustee's activity because the board as a policy-making body needs to approve the idea of starting a planned giving program. Second, the board must authorize a feasibility study. Is this planned giving program legal? What federal and state laws must be considered? When I speak of state laws, I mean those of *all* fifty states and not only those of the state of your incorporation.

Two additional considerations are (1) the age of your institution and (2) the future of your institution.

First, if your institution is just beginning, the opportunity for receiving very many giving contracts, such as gift annuities and trusts, will be limited. If your institution is over twenty years old and its work has been recognized as necessary and good, you could have a great opportunity. There is something about the age of an institution that gives a donor confidence— especially a planned giving donor.

Now, for the second consideration—*the future of your institu-*

tion. If yours is an educational institution, a welfare agency, a denomination, or a religious group with a large following, you probably will enjoy reasonable success. If you represent the second generation of a program that was started by a strong natural leader, it is possible that he gave little attention to planning for the future when he would no longer be around. In such an institution a planned giving program would suffer. This is especially true when this strong natural leader was, through the years, made the center of the donor's attention.

An example of such a person might be a great preacher whose name is recognized in every home, or a successful social worker who captured the imagination of all the lives he or she touched. In fairness to the strong natural leader, I must say this: The institution he brings into being *can have* an excellent and durable planned giving program if he plans it carefully while he is living—while he is known so well to so many.

The next step is to review the bylaws and the constitution. If everything checks out, then the board is made aware of the cost and the time required in a program. It takes time to get results; it takes perseverance to be able to wait for success. The board needs to know these facts.

Once the board of trustees has approved the idea of having a planned giving program and has authorized and completed a feasibility study, it is time for the *market survey*. This is done to produce a donor profile (see Chapter 3).

When drawing conclusions about your donor market, from which you derive your income, you cannot afford to guess; you need to have the best information possible. In addition to approving the planned giving program, it is essential that each board member becomes involved personally. The first objective should be to ask every board member to personally consider the planned giving options. Any member of the board of trustees is a potential planned giver.

Developing and Marketing Your Program

Now let us assume you have a fine, workable, approved plan. If it is not properly developed, the end result is *nothing*. So let's talk about developing and marketing the plan.

The Three Functions

The development function can be divided into three general areas: (1) *public relations,* (2) *marketing,* and (3) *counseling.*

Public Relations

In public relations we first consider how we will introduce the program to our constituency. Will we do it through letters, through news releases, or through continuous promotion of certain giving ideas? Will we advertise? At this point, I think we have to be prepared to manage the use of as many of these means as possible. *Public relations* is what you do *before asking* for the gift. *Asking* for the gift is *marketing* or *development.*

Before a public relations thrust is made, it is wise for the management to position its institution in the minds of its prospects. I am not referring to the image of your institution. I am talking about who you are—really. Do they know what your people *do* for other people? Can you say who you are in one word, a few words, or a sentence? When you hear IBM, what do you think of? Typewriters? Computers? Dairy products? What about NCR? Alcoa? General Motors?

Is your "in-house" language (use of initials, abbreviations, jargon, acronyms) adversely affecting your communication with your donors? Are you confusing them or causing them to draw a blank with your public relations thrust? If you know *who* you are and if you are convinced you can tell other people clearly who you are, then you are ready to start developing your program.

Use of articles. We often recommend starting the public relations thrust with an article in the institution's publication. This could be written by the chief executive officer to introduce the whole idea of planned giving as a service to the donors of the institution. The article should also introduce the planned giving director and offer friends of the institution his or her services by letter, phone, or personal visit when traveling in that area.

This could be followed up with a letter from the same executive indicating that friends of the institution will be receiving helpful information periodically, such as the enclosed

69

brochure on the subject of will making, which he feels may be of help to them in their personal financial planning. (See Chapter 9 for samples of material on wills.) Similar letters, articles, and ads can be used with the mailings of each giving plan.

An article on the importance of an individual's will could then appear in the next newsletter. A space ad focusing on wills and offering a free booklet on request could be placed in this issue also.

The wills approach has worked effectively for many institutions, and it is the initial approach the Planned Giving Institute usually recommends. However, it certainly is not the only way.

Testimonials. One group started its planned giving program with an article on how the first gift annuity came to the institution. In a newsletter to more than thirty thousand donors, a story told of an elderly couple who had given a substantial amount through a gift annuity. A photograph of the couple was used to illustrate the story. Here was a vivid testimonial of how one elderly couple had taken the opportunity to make an outstanding gift and at the same time provide additional financial security for themselves for the balance of their lives.

This is an excellent use of the personal testimony, one of the most powerful tools in public relations and advertising. In your publication, write about *special donors* who are following *specific programs of giving* to your institution. Let your readers take their cue from the motivation you have provided, and then give them an opportunity to request more information on the particular giving plan highlighted in the article.

Over the past several years, similar stories and articles have appeared in the newsletter of that institution each quarter. It has helped current donors increase their confidence in the institution and provide a plan for prospective donors to give to that institution on a long-range basis.

Advertising plan. In addition to the publicity program, this institution had a good advertising plan. They have run space ads in their newsletters and annual reports offering free brochures and booklets on wills, gift annuities, and so on.

Even as I was writing this material I received a telephone call from a client about how to assist a $50,000 gift annuity prospect who wanted to fund the gift annuity with highly appreciated securities. He also wanted to know the effective yield from a 7.5 percent rate of payment for a person in a 62 percent tax bracket. This lead came from a simple brochure mailed by our client institution.

Marketing

So far we have been "prospecting." Now we come to the actual marketing. Selling the planned giving approach during an interview is of prime importance. We become aware of our prospects through their inquiries. Generally, these are in the form of completed coupons, with the inquirer's date of birth included. These should be responded to immediately, if possible the same day the inquiry is received. Full information on the plan of giving requested by the prospect should be provided.

About ten days later, the inquirer should be called on the telephone. From this conversation a determination can be made as to the quality of the inquiry and whether or not a visit is in order. In this field, personal visits are necessary to insure proper explanation of the planned giving arrangements. A specialist in planned giving is a vital person if an institution is to have a successful planned giving program.

Counseling

If it is determined that the inquirer is a serious prospect, the representative should visit the home and *counsel* with the prospect. The planned giving officer should listen to what the prospect wants to do and assist him in arriving at goals and plans to implement those goals. This often means providing coordination for a complete estate planning project, making it necessary for the planned giving officer to work with one or more members of the estate planning team.

The estate planning team. The attorney of the prospective donor should be brought into the picture very soon, especially if contracts are involved. The attorney can become a vital part of

71

the interviewing and counseling process. If trusts seem to be advisable, then a trust officer should be brought in to help.

When a large estate is being analyzed, often the donor's accountant, who has all the donor's financial records, is vital in the planning stage. If much life insurance is involved, the donor's life insurance agent should be contacted. If royalty agreements or special kinds of oil leases and real estate are in the estate, then other specialists should be brought in for consultation.

When the members of the estate planning team finish their work, a completed estate plan will have been created for the donor. Now, if the prospective donor whose estate has been analyzed is able to make a charitable gift and include it in his estate plan, we can refer to this whole process as *charitable estate planning*.

The goal of a planned giving officer should be to get involved in as many estate analysis situations as possible. This often means that the donor will include that institution for a substantial part, or maybe all, of the estate at his or her death.

Managing Your Planned Giving Program

If we make careful plans and develop those plans properly, then we have a *management function* that is continuous.

Institutions can become one-sided in their thinking. Some leaders are concerned only with their *mission*. They are very strongly and exclusively oriented toward accomplishing their institution's mission. This sounds great on first hearing. But I am convinced that to have a balanced picture, institutional managers must equalize the mission affairs (your mission is why you exist), the business affairs, and the public affairs of the institution. (See Table 3 on page 73.)

For example, business affairs include the proper management of the people working behind the scenes. These people conserve the gifts entrusted to the institution for the support of those carrying out the mission of the institution. Public affairs include relating to the public by keeping them informed and by seeking gifts to keep the mission activity moving ahead. And, of course, mission affairs involve carrying out the organization's purpose. Table 3 below shows the possible placement of these officers within the organizational structure.

Four areas of management are involved in a planned giving program: personnel, investments, systems, and communication.

TABLE 3
SAMPLE ORGANIZATIONAL CHART

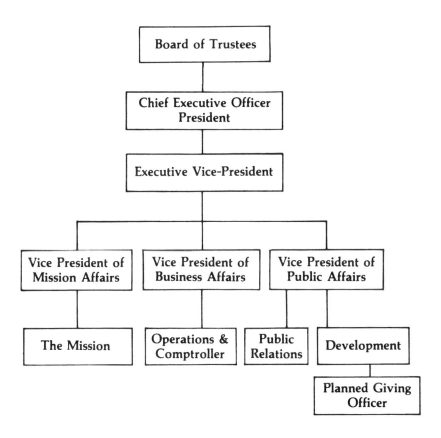

Personnel

Once the program is on the move, and the marketing process is working and producing leads and interviews, then consider

adding field staff and office help. You need to be sure that once you throw out the line you will be able to pull in the catch. Unfortunately, except for the more simple planned gifts, such as bequests, gift annuities, and life insurance, most of your prime prospects cannot be dealt with by standard methods and procedures. Once a qualified prospect is obtained, give him great personal attention.

One complication to be avoided is introducing new personnel into negotiations that have been in progress for some time. Once negotiations with a prospective donor are begun with a given representative(s) of your institution, the parties to the negotiation process *should not be changed or added to*—except in the case of needing additional professionals.

Each planned giver requires the time of your top-level staff. Therefore negotiations with new prospects should be delayed until proper attention can be devoted to them.

No segment of the field of fund raising demands more intimate knowledge of the prospect list than planned gifts. Obviously, everything possible must be known about those who make up this group of important donors. Intimate details are to be known and recorded, along with letters expressing gratitude. Notes should be made and filed immediately following every visit or telephone conversation. Above all, the information should be accurate and kept highly confidential.

Investments

Perhaps the most important function in management is the investment of other people's money. The financial officer or the staff person delegated to handle these matters should exercise great care to see that annuity funds are properly invested in a well diversified, segregated portfolio, or that gift annuities are insured by a life insurance company.

The financial officer will need to seek counsel on investments and not be placed in the position of making one-man investment decisions in this highly complicated area of finance. An annuity account should be invested to produce fixed income. It would probably *not* be prudent to invest annuity reserves in mutual funds or in a portfolio where the major investment is common stocks. The fund should be well-balanced. It could be quality stocks and bonds with emphasis on yield, safety of principal, and marketability. A unitrust or pooled income fund could be invested with a high emphasis on growth. Remember, these trustee-type investments are a sacred trust. Careless handling of investments can hurt your own institution, your donors, and other institutions working in the planned giving area.

The development officer needs to eliminate friction and have the best cooperation possible from the financial officer. The one in charge of management of the funds and the administration of the contracts must be a very strong ally.

Systems

Do you have a filing system that *works* for you, or *frustrates* you? When referring to systems, I am referring to fund raising files generally and planned giving files specifically. I am also referring to the follow-up after an agreement has been made and to the settling of wills and other agreements after the death of the donor.

First, let's look at the donor lists. Have the donors been classified? Study the chart on page 76. This is a sample filing system. This system can be used whether you have computer capability or a three- by five-inch card system. The dollar amounts listed under the "Current Donor Program" section of the chart can be changed to suit your donors' giving patterns.

All good fund raising programs have a way of bringing new names into the files. These go into the *name* section. Once a gift is made, the name is moved into the appropriate category. After careful solicitation of a name, if no gift is received, it is moved into the *inactive* file. When the person gives, you have a program of maintenance and upgrading. The goal is to retain the donor and to motivate and encourage him to give more.

Experience has taught us that the best prospects for planned gifts are current donors; therefore, it is best to direct one's efforts toward them. There is always the possibility that nondonors

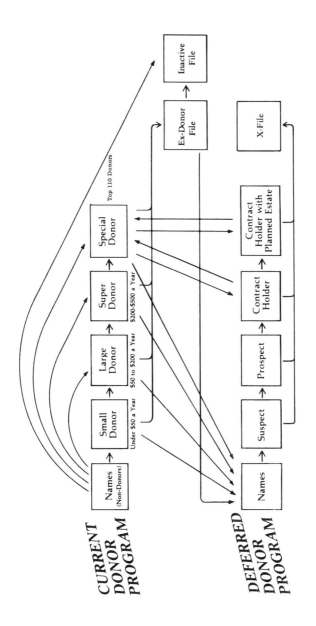

TABLE 4
SAMPLE FILING SYSTEM

will make planned gifts, but do not put great emphasis on seeking them out.

When starting a planned giving program, approach donors in all categories. If the list is large, use a test program to learn where your best prospects will come from.

If a person responds for any reason, his name goes into the *suspect* file. Then, if through mail and telephone and personal contacts you determine that the "suspect" shows promise, move the name into the *prospect* file. After interviewing, if you close a planned giving arrangement, move the name into the *contract-holder* file. If through further contact you begin an *estate analysis* with the person, move the name to that section of the files. If at any time in the process you find a person is not interested, move the name to the *inactive* file.

Usually the largest donors (the special donor category on the chart) are the best prospects for estate analysis, and consequently those same donors often become some of your better prospects for planned gift arrangements.

It is essential to follow-up on all contract holders and those who have gone through estate analysis. The best prospects for planned gifts are those who have already made them. These people will sometimes refer you to friends or relatives who might also make planned giving arrangements.

When a contract, trust, or will is to be paid to the institution, careful follow-up with lawyers, courts, executors, banks, and personal representatives of the deceased can often speed up delivery of the funds to your institution.

Communication

It is necessary to carefully manage the communication of planned giving ideas to your donors. By communication, I mean telling your donor family clearly, simply, and frequently the benefits of giving through such means as wills, gift annuities, and trusts. What needs to be managed is the content of the printed material mailed from your institution. The copy needs to be legally correct, although written in a nonlegal way. A single mailing each year is of little value. A well-conceived plan of three or four mailings each year is necessary. Ideally, these mailings should be supported with newsletters or magazine articles and advertisements.

If you plan carefully, develop and market diligently, and manage prudently, you will have an excellent opportunity to succeed in your planned giving efforts.

Chapter Seven
The Ways People
Give—Now

Back when our country was young, and bartering was a common system of exchange, money may have been one of the least likely items one would consider giving. If someone was in need, a neighbor would give food from his garden, timber from his land, or flour from his mill.

In today's economy, however, though we may still take food to a sick neighbor, cash is the most convenient charitable gift. Cash can be exchanged for whatever is needed most, whether it is medicine, food, books, or workers' salaries.

People sometimes complain about appeals for cash. One nettled citizen saved all his direct mail appeals for cash over a month's time and weighed them—just to prove that his grumbling was justified. Calls for "help" weighed twelve pounds.

Another person complained to a popular newspaper columnist that if he gave to every cause asking for help he and his wife would surely soon be in the poor house. The columnist replied that since America is such a land of givers, if this disgruntled one did become destitute, others would no doubt be there to meet his needs. The conclusion was that we should be glad we are still on the giving end.

At any rate, Americans are giving away tens of billions of dollars each year. And I believe most are doing it because of their own need to give. I am convinced most people enjoy giving.

Now Giving

When we speak of "now" giving, we are referring to any kind of gift made right now for current or future use. A giver makes a current gift in response to regular or special appeals for support, through capital campaigns, and annual fund drives.

Direct mail is the most commonly used means of appeal, but there are also banquets (see Appendix 1), efforts of volunteers, telethons, and personal presentations to individuals or to foundation boards by officers of the institution.

When pledges from capital campaigns are paid, they become "now" gifts. When a planned gift matures and comes into the account of the institution, at that point it becomes a "now" gift.

Every gift becomes a "now" gift at some point.

An institution that expects to have a successful *planned* giving program must build from a successful *now* giving program. An effective current giving program is based on a list of prospective donors with a plan for developing these names until they either become donors or are eliminated from the file. Such a program also includes specific plans for maintaining and upgrading the donor to a higher or more frequent giving pattern.

Keeping Your Givers

Here are some "ground rules" to help you keep your "now" givers *current* and growing:

- Give name acquisition a high priority. Make it a daily activity. Every employee should use every means possible to add names daily to the prospective donor list. Present donors should be solicited at least once each year for names of friends—people with the same kinds of interests as theirs. Some institutions purchase names they can use to locate donors.

- Prospective donors must be *asked* to give and may be approached by mail, by telephone, by personal face-to-face contact on a one-to-one basis, or they can be invited to a seminar or other type of group meeting.

- Once a person has made the first gift, a plan of communication should be developed. This plan can include a periodic newsletter (at least quarterly) to donors. The purpose of this newsletter is to inform donors of how their gifts are being used and to give information supporting present or future fund raising projects. The newsletter should create a climate for giving by helping people feel good about the gifts they have already made and confident about the gifts they will make in the future. This newsletter is an ideal vehicle for keeping your planned giving opportunities before the donor family.

• Frequent direct-mail appeals to donors will keep the financial and service aspects of the institution before the people.

Direct-mail appeals are usually built around a letter, one to four pages in length, perhaps focusing on a person or a group of people who represent those served by the institution. The need is described and identified as one of many; the solution is suggested in monetary terms; a deadline is named to give the letter a "do it now" flavor; a reply card and business-reply envelope are enclosed. There may also be a brochure giving further emphasis to the need if a special project is underway, or the brochure might give general information about the institution.

Such mailings could go out each month. Whether or not this overloads the constituents is a matter for testing. Your constituents will let you know if they can take an appeal a month by their response in giving. You may find that six mailings a year are best for you.

If you don't know where to start, you might try one appeal per quarter, and then increase to six times a year if the response is favorable.

Some institutions so resist the idea of asking for money that they never actually plan ahead for appeal mailings. They simply let finances get to the crisis stage and then call for friends to save the ship—and this happens year after year.

Why not go ahead and plan annual mailings to prevent the crises and thus allow for wiser planning of available funds? It *is* possible to anticipate needs, present a solid, positive opportunity to have a part in a great work, and provide the prospective giver a convenient way to respond.

- At least once each year, a personal "thank you" should go from the chief executive officer, either by letter, by telephone, or by personal visit to all who have given. An annual report should be a regular part of the communication plan. An annual report can be in brochure or booklet form, giving highlights of the year, a message of thanks from the chief executive, a brief financial report and summary of the year's activities—plus other information and photos to describe the institution's work.
- The telephone should be used freely in asking for certain gifts and for making appointments.
- Fund raising banquets can be used successfully in areas where there are large segments of your donors. Don't overlook having a donor appreciation banquet to report back, to thank them, to get them together for valuable esprit de corps building.
- Check up on people who have quit giving. Plan your files so that the names of people who have not given in six months or a year are brought to your attention; if they had an established pattern of giving and suddenly stopped giving, write or call them to ask why. Tell them you have missed their gifts; ask if anything is wrong. This kind of activity will do more for your institution than you might imagine. To conserve a donor is of greater value than finding a new one!

Other Ideas

Any appeal for "now" gifts is also an opportunity to suggest other ways of giving, such as suggesting gifts of securities, life insurance, property, etc.

Every institution will vary its approach because of its own characteristics and its market. For example, an *educational institution* may have a program for parents, an alumni program, and a community program. It may be related to a denomination with potential support from church budgets.

A *hospital* has its staff of doctors, nurses, and other personnel (we know of one hospital that has some six thousand employees) plus patients, former patients, and the volunteer auxiliary. In some cases churches may also be involved as well as the general community.

A *religious institution* develops its donors based on their commitment to a particular philosophy or a good work being done. Many who give are those who have benefited from the work of the institution.

One thing for sure: No two institutions are identical and none should copy another institution's approach. Each fund raising program should be unique to that particular institution and show its own "personality."

Two Now-Giving Options Overlooked

There are two now-giving opportunities most donors never hear about because the institutions to which they give never have planned for such gifts and do not know how to receive them. I speak of giving through *life insurance* and *securities*.

Life Insurance Policies

Certain types of life insurance gifts are uncomplicated and, to be received, would not require constitutional changes, board approval, or management conferences by most institutions. Such gifts are given outright with no contracts and no future involvement.

Life insurance is generally thought of as a death benefit paid to a beneficiary to replace the dollars lost when a person dies. It is interesting to note that more dollars are paid out by life insurance companies as a result of maturing endowments, annual dividends, annuity payments, and cash surrenders than as death benefits.

Giving an endowment policy. An *endowment policy* is a cash value policy. The premiums are paid for a certain number of years, usually ten, fifteen, twenty, or thirty years or to age 65. If the policyholder dies, the face amount is paid, but if he lives until the end of the term of years specified, the policy proceeds are paid to the policyholder in cash. For example, a twenty-year endowment provides $10,000 of life insurance protection for twenty years and at the end of twenty years, $10,000 is returned to the policyowner.

You may effectively ask a potential donor these questions or bring them to his attention through a letter, brochure, or article in your in-house publication:

• Do you have one of those small policies for $500, $1,000, or $2,000 that your parents bought when you were a child? Do you really need it today? Why not give it?

• Do you have a policy on your life that was intended to protect your wife or husband who died, a child who is grown, or a mortgage already paid? Why not give it?

• Do you have a policy you bought to pay for your children's education? Or do you have paid-up endowments you don't really need? Why not give them?

• Do you have a retirement-type life insurance policy you no longer need because you have been able to provide for your retirement through unanticipated prosperity? Why not give it?

Giving dividends. Your donors can assign annual policy dividends to your institution. Most life insurance is purchased on a dividend (participating) basis. A $15,000 policy may pay a dividend of $50 the first year and as much as $100 the tenth year. You should urge people to assign their life insurance policy dividends to your institution.

EXAMPLE: A person, age 40, purchasing a $15,000 policy from one leading company would pay $417.60 in premiums. The dividend projected for the first year is $45.60, while the twentieth year dividend is estimated to be $180.75. The total dividends for twenty years would be $2,197.00 or $109.85 average per year. This is a substantial gift. When the donor assigns his dividends to your institution, he sets in motion an annual gift plan that could continue for life.

Life insurance policy dividends are not reportable as income for tax purposes. When one of your donors assigns life insurance policy dividends to your institution, the dividend is deductible as a gift. (Other ways of giving life insurance are described in Chapter 10.)

How to receive life insurance gifts. A sample letter (see Table 5) may be suggested to your prospective giver as a means for setting in motion his or her gift of life insurance. The donor's life insurance company, on receipt of such a letter from your donor, should be responsible for transferring the policy to your institution as owner and beneficiary. The policy may then be cashed in by your institution at the proper time.

TABLE 5
SAMPLE LETTER TO LIFE INSURANCE COMPANY

Name of insurance company
Street
City, State, Zip

Refer to policy #_____

Please send me necessary papers to make a charitable gift of life insurance benefits to (Name of institution), a not-for-profit corporation.

Send the following:
- ☐ I would like to assign my policy dividends.
- ☐ I would like to name (Institution) as
  - ☐ Primary beneficiary
  - ☐ Secondary beneficiary
  - ☐ Final beneficiary
  - ☐ For a percent of proceeds
- ☐ I would like to transfer policy ownership to (Institution) irrevocably.
- ☐ I would like to purchase a new policy naming (Institution) as the owner and beneficiary.
- ☐ I would like to name (Institution) as remainder beneficiary in my _____ annuity _____ supplementary contract should I die before receiving all payments guaranteed.

Signed

Stocks and Bonds, Including Mutual Funds

Your donors can give securities to your institution now. They don't have to wait until you have a sophisticated program and a full-time planned giving staff.

In the years that I have been encouraging donors to give securities and reminding my clients to ask for gifts of securities, the results have been most gratifying.

One donor told me he was planning to give $1,000 to a certain charitable institution. I asked him if he owned any securities that had appreciated in value. He did have 100 shares of stock valued at nearly $2,500 that had cost him only $500 originally.

Even though this man was a professional he didn't know he could give securities, and he didn't know the institution wanted them. This prospective donor decided to give all the stock. The briefest mention that he could give stocks prompted him to increase his gift by two-and-a-half times.

Tax reasons for giving securities. Under present (1978) tax laws, when a person owns securities longer than twelve months and gives them outright to your institution, they are received at the current fair market value. The donor is able to deduct as a gift on his federal income tax return the full fair market value of the securities and he avoids all capital gains tax. (As you read, remember that tax laws may be changed at any time. Keep abreast of any current tax information supplied by the federal government.)

EXAMPLES: Mr. Wilson bought one-hundred shares of the XYZ Corporation common stock for $1,000 four years ago. The fair market value of this stock is now $5,000. He has an unrealized capital gain of $4,000. If he made a pledge of $5,000 to your institution, he could simply transfer the stock to your institution, satisfy his pledge, and deduct $5,000 as a charitable contribution on his federal income tax return, paying no capital gains taxes.

Mr. Brown bought one hundred shares of XYZ Corporation stock for $1,000. It is now worth $5,000. He decides to make a gift of stock to your institution on the "bargain sale" arrangement. He offers to sell this one hundred shares of stock to your charity for his original cost of $1,000. He is able to deduct $4,000 on his income tax return as a gift to your institution while reporting only a portion of the realized capital gains as income.

Mr. Jones owns one hundred shares of stock in the Ajax Corporation, which cost him $5,000 four years ago. The stock decreased in value and is now worth only $3,000. Rather than give the stock to your institution, he sells it himself, gives the $3,000 to your institution and takes an income tax deduction for that amount. He reports the long-term capital loss against his gains on his income tax return. It is very important to know the cost basis of any shares of stock you receive from a donor. You should help him get as much tax advantage as possible from his gift of stock.

Giving more at no greater cost. Let's say that Mr. Morgan is in a 20 percent income tax bracket and is considering a $1,000 gift (from his current income) to your institution. If he keeps the $1,000 he will have to pay a tax of $200 on it. Therefore, the $1,000 is worth only $800 to him in spendable income. If he makes a gift to your institution, you receive the $1,000, but it only costs Mr. Morgan $800 to make the gift. The government, in effect, pays the other $200 since Mr. Morgan can deduct the $1,000 on his tax return at the 20 percent level.

On the other hand, Mr. Fitzhugh, who is in the 50 percent bracket, could make the same $1,000 gift to your institution at a cost of only $500 to him. Thus our tax system encourages people with more money to give more. A friend already considering an annual gift of $500, for instance, might increase his gift and enjoy the giving experience even more. If Mr. Morgan or Mr. Fitzhugh will give appreciated securities, the actual cost of their gifts will be further reduced.

One in seven Americans, or about one in three families, or as many as 32 million people own securities. Undoubtedly, if the people who make up your constituency have above average income and education, most of them will more than likely own some kind of securities. These may be mutual funds, regular company stock, corporate bonds, municipal bonds, certain government bonds, or even church bonds.

Short-term capital gains. When appreciated securities held less than twelve months are given to a charitable organization, the amount permitted for a tax deduction is limited to the original cost of the security.

In planning your appeal for funds each year, try to get across to your donors the various ways they can give securities to your institution. One institution started asking for gifts of stocks, and within two years it was receiving three times as many gifts of stock as it had received in previous years.

Know how to receive gifts of securities. The donor can ask his broker to transfer the stock certificate into the name of your institution. . . .

OR

The donor can be asked to complete the stock certificate on the reverse side and sign it exactly as his name appears on the face of the stock certificate. He should always have a broker or banker guarantee the signature. . . .

OR

The donor can send your institution an unsigned stock certificate in one envelope and the assignment agreement, or what is commonly called a stock power, in another envelope. This stock power should also be signed and guaranteed by a bank or broker. . . .

OR

Your donor can always write to the transfer agent and ask for advice on transferring stocks to your institution.

Your donors will give more stocks when you ask for them.

How to Encourage Gifts of Securities and Life Insurance

A similar approach may be taken in attracting either of these types of gifts. The best approach is a direct mailing (i.e., a letter, newsletter, or in house publication) to all of your donors.

Use articles in your newsletter or magazine (if these are available) and place space ads at the same time. The articles could be built around people who have already made gifts of securities or life insurance to your institution, or about people who gave to their own "favorite charity" this way. Both articles and ads should offer more information on the plan of giving featured.

Follow-up articles might take a question-answer format, or they could present real or simulated interviews between your planned giving director and friends of the institution.

At least annually, mail out brochures on ways to give stocks and life insurance. When you write to a donor about giving, include a paragraph or even a postscript on the value of giving stocks or life insurance policies.

In telephone solicitations, tell the donor who owns appreciated securities it may be to his advantage to give securities instead of cash. Or remind him that small paid-up life insurance policies make convenient gifts without affecting current income.

All development staff members and the chief executive officer should be well-informed about these two giving ideas.

Although we have gone into some detail in this chapter, I am aware that we have not fully covered the subject of now-giving programs for the nonprofit institution. My purpose in mentioning the now-giving program at all is to set the stage for the planned giving effort. Current giving leads to planned giving.

Before discussing giving through wills and contract giving plans, we will take a look at the way a planned giving program can become an asset to the present support of your institution.

Chapter Eight
The Planned Giving
Rationale

Many administrators of nonprofit institutions have a "bird in the hand" philosophy. They are more concerned with immediate gifts than with later ones. In fact, they are so wrapped up with meeting this month's quota—or this year's—that they don't even have time to consider what they will be getting next year, much less what they will need five or ten years hence.

They fail to take the long-range view. Some believe that a planned giving program is too indefinite and complicated, with the pay-off too far in the future. The whole idea seems like a wispy, blue-sky concept, unworthy of serious consideration.

"After all," they explain, "we need gifts *now*. Next year will have to take care of itself." It's a shame so many have this attitude, because *immediate gifts are invariably much smaller than deferred ones.* And this view tends to chain them to a hand-to-mouth treadmill. They fall into the trap of asking for too little— too urgently and too soon.

The Relationship Between
Planned Giving and Now Gifts

The old idea that "a bird in the hand is worth two in the bush" just isn't valid here. The risk alluded to in that adage does not exist in planned giving. You don't have to drop, lose, or even endanger the small immediate gift in order to get the large future one. In fact, *discussing planned gifts with donors often increases immediate gifts* as an incidental by-product of securing the planned ones.

The Planned Giving Rationale

A well-devised planned giving program can bring you both the "bird in the hand" and the "two in the bush," only more often it's six or eight or ten "in the bush." A quality planned giving program is geared to reach both former donors and current small, large, and super donors.

EXAMPLES: Mrs. Browder, a widow of moderate means, was visited by the development director of the small church-related college she had attended years earlier. At various times over the years she had given small sums during the college's annual fund drive—$25, $50, or $100. The development director asked her to consider a larger gift this year.

"I guess I could spare $250," said Mrs. Browder. "But I only have a small income from Social Security and a few investments my late husband made. No telling how much I would need if I became seriously ill. I can't endanger my security. My resources are so limited. Let me think it over."

A few months later the development director saw Mrs. Browder again. During the interim the college had established a planned giving program. On this call the director asked her to remember the college in her will, and to help in the current drive as much as she could. He received not only the $250 immediate gift discussed earlier—the "bird in hand"—but also a $10,000 bequest when Mrs. Browder died two years later.

Mrs. Miller was called on by the executive secretary of one of several missionary groups she supported. This group did not have a planned giving program. The executive asked for an immediate gift to meet an immediate need. Mrs. Miller assured him that $300 was the best she could do, and she gave him a check. He left pleased with the feeling that he had received as large a gift as she could spare. And he had.

But two weeks later the head of another missionary group with a planned giving program called on Mrs. Miller.

"I've just given a rather large amount to another missionary group," she said. "I really can't spare another single dollar right now."

"That's all right," said the executive. "I don't want to talk about that anyway. I want to talk about a future gift, and I particularly want to show you several ways you might arrange now to give later and, in so doing, perhaps cut your taxes this year and even increase your present and future income."

This isn't doubletalk. It's done every day. It's possible through any of several standard giving plans.

When the executive director left, he believed he would eventually see the bulk of Mrs. Miller's estate come to his mission society. When she died a few years later, they received almost $25,000. Wouldn't the first missionary executive have been surprised—and somewhat chagrined—to know that?

There are several lessons here:

1. Many people who honestly can't afford large immediate gifts can afford deferred gifts.

2. Most people don't mind giving money that isn't actually released until after they no longer need it.

3. Planned gifts don't endanger an individual's security; on the contrary, they can strengthen it.

Psychological Advantages of the Planned Giving Approach

Many people who seemingly are stingy (or at least parsimonious) are often remarkably generous when deciding how their wealth is to be distributed after death. During life, people usually give only the "extra" money they can "spare." But they know that after they die there will be no such categories. It will *all* be extra money they can spare—money that has to be disbursed. The only questions are *how* and *to whom*.

So here you have the two greatest advantages of a planned giving program: (1) Planned gifts are usually larger than now gifts, and (2) now gifts and planned gifts are *not* mutually exclusive. There is no need to give up the former for the latter.

This brings other advantages. Your fund raising efforts are stabilized; your campaign has a broader base. As planned gifts pick up momentum, you have occasional breathing spells for thinking and planning even farther ahead.

You also find that planned gifts are usually easier to obtain, even though they are larger. There are several psychological factors that make this so.

The Distant Future

First, you have the advantage of "the unreal future." The future *is* unreal. It always seems farther away than it actually is. Next month seems like next year, while last month seems like yesterday. The year 2000 seems dazzlingly futuristic, yet it was no farther away in 1978 in a forward direction than 1956 was in a backward one. Most of us will live to see it. Intellectually, it's an obvious fact. But emotionally it remains incredibly far off.

So people often agree to give more in the apparently distant future than they would consider giving today. People also assume the future will be more prosperous than the present, for it usually is. This assumption is the very foundation of our national economy today—our enjoy-now-pay-later credit system. So the future gift is further enlarged.

The Pressure Is Off

When you talk in terms of future giving, you take the pressure off. This is another psychological factor in your favor. The donor knows you don't expect to pin him down or get a check right away, so the discussion is more relaxed. Because of this atmosphere, you can deal with higher figures without anyone getting tense. It is easier for the donor to give future gifts and easier for you to ask for them.

Sacrifice Is Postponed

Giving usually requires sacrifice, but planned giving postpones it—often to a point where it's no sacrifice at all. Giving without sacrifice is a compellingly attractive idea. It's easier to promise to give later than to actually give now. And by projection, it's easier to give a lot at a later time than to give a little now.

You are asking the donor to think about the totality of his possessions—what will eventually become of them and what might be done with them after his death. You are also, inevitably, talking in terms of thousands, or perhaps tens of thousands, or more.

And you are pointing out to your donor certain tax advantages and savings provided by various methods of planned giving and advising him to discuss them with his attorney or trust officer or tax advisor.

The Planned Giving Program and the Institution's Image

A planned giving program enhances the stature of your own institution. It puts it in the same league with the nation's biggest and most prestigious hospitals, universities, churches, and religious organizations. It adds sophistication to your institutional position in your donor's mind. It indirectly tells your donor that your institution is more solid than those year-to-year, hand-to-mouth fund seekers, and that you are making plans far ahead for an exciting and purposeful future.

A planned giving program helps you penetrate the growing public resistance to fund raising appeals. Fund raisers are today being scrutinized, criticized, and regulated as never before. Some of the public say they are weary of appeals. They appear to be more resistant to them, more aware of the built-in costs of fund raising, more skeptical about the merit of good causes, more selective in giving, more ready to say "no" or "not this time" or "I'm giving already to too many other things." A planned giving program helps carry you over this hurdle because it is a service that gives the donor many benefits in return, and this service is offered by only a small percentage of the institutions seeking funds.

Meeting this "competition" effectively is your biggest challenge today. *The New York Times* estimates that over fifty million volunteers per year ask for contributions for one cause or another. *Time* magazine says there are nine to eleven drives in progress simultaneously on any given day in the average city. There were over two thousand United Fund campaigns last year alone. *Newsweek* has reported that many leading New York businessmen receive invitations to twenty-five different charity functions within an average two-week period. And all this is happening despite the prodigious growth of government programs to aid worthy people and institutions.

Planned Giving and Current Trends

A planned giving program by your institution can benefit from several helpful current trends.

First, the national economy is growing. People have more money than ever before—to spend, to save, and to leave when they die. This prosperity is more widespread than ever before.

Second, the standard of living is rising for almost everyone. Historically, good times have been good primarily for the wealthy. But tax and social service legislation and social trends have redistributed much wealth. More elderly people are prosperous today than ever before. Social Security and Medicare have made it possible for millions of people, who would have died destitute as recently as 1960, to leave small estates today. And "small" really means fairly large. The government considers any estate under $134,000 in 1978 and $175,000 in 1981 and thereafter too small to incur federal estate taxes. But most fund raisers would consider a gift of half those amounts quite substantial indeed. So there is more potential for planned gifts than ever before.

Third, the average life expectancy of the population has increased. People are living longer and dying older. In most cases, this means they have more to leave to older children who need it less—thus freeing more funds for worthy institutions.

Types of Planned Gifts

There are many types of planned gifts sought and received by charitable, religious, and educational institutions—some simple and some complex. Here are some brief descriptions.

Bequests

These are, of course, gifts left by will. This is the best known planned gift, and therefore the most often used. Wills are readily understood, and most people recognize a will as a personal responsibility; therefore, charitable bequests are easily "marketable."

Securities

These are gifts of stocks and bonds. They offer donors special tax advantages. If a stock has increased in value, the donor gives the stock itself and avoids paying taxes on the increase. If the stock has decreased in value, the donor sells it and donates the proceeds in order to apply the capital loss of value against his other income to reduce his taxes. A "bargain sale" of a stock that has increased in value returns the donor's original cost and gives the increase to the institution.

In all cases the gift is deductible by the donor as a charitable contribution. The recipient institution needs no special staff or expertise to handle it. Many people are smart enough to buy stocks that increase in value but are not informed sufficiently to know they can give the stock instead of cash.

Life Insurance

There are many types of life insurance gifts. A donor can give the dividends on a policy or make your institution primary, secondary, or final beneficiary. He may simply transfer the ownership of a policy no longer needed or purchase a new policy for your institution's benefit or purchase life insurance to cover a pledge or bequest to your institution. For instance, if a donor makes a pledge of $10,000 to your institution, he may want to purchase a new life insurance policy in that amount to guarantee the $10,000 gift in case of his prior death.

Trusts

This is a method of setting aside property to be administered by trustees for the benefit of the donor and your institution. The "setting aside" can provide certain tax advantages. A trust can be short-term, revocable, or irrevocable. The tax advantages vary according to type. Trust gifts are very common, popular, and helpful to both donors and recipient institutions.

Gift Annuities

A donor gives a stated sum to the institution in exchange for an agreement that guarantees annual payments to the donor for life. At death, the remaining annuity funds become a gift to the institution. Amount of payment is determined by the age of the donor-annuitant and the schedule of rates in use by the charitable institution at the time the gift is made. The donor gets a federal income tax deduction the year the agreement becomes effective and most of the annuity payments are tax free if the beneficiaries are 50 years of age or older. (Donors often exchange appreciated stocks for gift annuities.) Before beginning a gift annuity program, the institution should be aware of certain permit requirements of some states.

Life Estate Contracts

A donor gives the institution real estate (a family farm or personal residence), retaining the right to use it the rest of his life. The real estate becomes the property of the institution by contract at the donor's death, thus bypassing probate court costs and certain other settlement costs. The donor is allowed a federal income tax deduction in the year the contract is made.

Pooled Income Funds

A number of donors place funds in a trust. Funds given are held in a trust, invested, and the interest or dividends are paid to the donor on a pro-rata basis. The income from this arrangement varies according to the return on the investment.

These very brief thumbnail descriptions are intended only to illustrate the wide variety of plans and programs your institution may offer.

Where Do You Start?

Resolve to avoid the three most common mistakes made by fund raisers who are pondering planned giving programs:

1. Don't assume you will receive planned gifts without asking for them. It rarely happens. Such gifts go almost always only to institutions that request them.

2. Don't assume that your faithful regular donors will give *you* planned gifts after receiving information about them

from *another* institution or organization. People invariably give to those who provide the basic information—yes, even when it's a new, young institution versus a grand old one that they have supported for years. That is why it's vital for you to get to your own loyal supporters first with planned giving information.

3. Don't assume you need a big staff or big budget or special expertise to launch a planned giving program. You don't need to cover the whole range immediately. If you can't afford a full-fledged program, there are simple types of planned gifts you can ask for and receive without special handling, follow-up, or problems.

You can start soliciting and receiving four of these gifts now: (1) bequests, (2) securities, (3) life insurance, and (4) real estate.[1] You can begin by setting up a year's calendar of mailings to your donors and prospects on the subject of bequests—as outlined in Chapter 9. You can offer information on other topics throughout the year, using space ads in your house publication and adding a paragraph or a postscript when you send any information that has been requested.

You can get this started now, and broaden your program when you are ready to hire a full-time planned giving officer to go into the field to visit your donors.

Of course, I can't guarantee unmitigated success for every planned giving program launched. But I can say this: I know of no institution anywhere, of any type, that regrets having undertaken a planned giving program.

Let me conclude with a few review words of caution: (1) Donors making planned gifts must be properly protected through a well-devised investment program; (2) adequate professional counsel should be used; (3) a budget sufficient to cover the program for three years is necessary; (4) a board and staff who can wait for results are a must.

---

[1]Even a local church can have an effective program covering these kinds of gifts. A "how-to-do-it" manual entitled "27 Ways to Increase Giving to Your Church" is available from Robert F. Sharpe and Company Inc. See page 285 for ordering information.

Chapter Nine
The Ways People
Give—Later
Part I: Wills

Arthur Agar was 74 years old when I first met him. He had retired at age 65 and had moved to another state. He had an adequate retirement plan and $75,000 in savings. He had no heirs.

He told me he started "dabbling" in real estate after retirement and had built his assets to more than $600,000 in houses, unimproved land, notes, mortgages, utility stocks, bonds, and savings and loan certificates of deposit. We discussed the use of trusts for management purposes and tax deductions.

But after much conversation he decided he would manage his property as long as he could, not worry about tax savings, and make a simple will—the ideal way for him to give.

Wills are better known to your donors than any other deferred giving plan. Yet while most people know about wills, *they often do not have a valid will.*

Several years ago one of the nation's leading news magazines carried an article on the subject of estate planning. It was written by four of the leading estate planners in the United States. One of the men was A. James Casner, former dean of the Harvard Law School. In this article Mr. Casner predicted that by the end of that year an average of *one hundred million dollars* a week would pile up in the probate courts because people were dying intestate (with no will) or leaving unclear or outdated wills.

Unfortunately, this prognostication came true and current

statistics show that literally millions of dollars continue to pile up in the probate courts daily. Recent surveys estimate that anywhere from 50 to 70 percent of all the individuals of adult age in the United States today die intestate or without a valid will.

(Our own experience with donor surveys indicates that more than 50 percent of the charitable givers who replied already had wills, well above the general public's average.)

From Wills to Bequests

As you consider wills, you are thinking of ways high-interest donors can be encouraged to name your institution for a share of their estates. However, too often planned giving officers send out charitable bequest information *before* they send out information encouraging the making of a will. But, of course, if a donor doesn't have a will, he cannot name your institution in it.

The best approach is first to encourage your donors to think of making their wills, and then to follow later by asking them to include your institution in their wills.

Because the will is the best known deferred giving plan, I believe it is the best approach to use to get the attention of people who may eventually place large sums in a trust, a gift annuity, or in some other more effective giving plan. I see the will as an important vehicle to help solve a person's need to give.

Let's define a will and a charitable bequest:

A will: The last will and testament is a legal document executed by a legally competent person during his lifetime, stating in writing whom he wants to get his property when he dies.

The person may arrange the provisions of the will in such a way that the beneficiary's right to the property may be unrestricted or restricted in some way. For example, he may leave his property to one person, subject to the right of another person to receive the income for a period of years or for life. The principal remaining at the death of the income beneficiary will

100

then be delivered to the final beneficiary who is the remainderman.

A charitable bequest: A gift of a certain amount, or a percent of an estate, or all or part of the residue of a will to be given to a qualified charitable institution at the death of a person.

Three Ways to Transfer Property

It is possible to transfer property at death by a *will*, by *law*, or by *contract*.

By Will

At the death of the testator (one who makes a will), it is the responsibility of the executor or the possessor of the will to take it to the probate court and offer it for proof as the last will and testament of the decedent. If the court is satisfied that the document presented is indeed the last will and testament of the decedent, the judge will name the executor as appointed in the will, if at all possible. ("Probate" means proving the validity of the will.)

The judge will instruct the executor to carry out his responsibilities of collecting the assets of the estate, paying any valid debts, expenses, and taxes. Then bequests are fulfilled as he makes distribution of the remaining assets. Most states require some kind of accounting from the executor in order to close the estate and relieve him of further jurisdiction from the probate court.

By Law

When you do not leave a will, the state has in effect made one for you! When a person fails to exercise his right to make a will and then dies, his property is distributed in accordance with the laws of descent and distribution. In other words, state legislatures have passed laws that govern who gets a person's property when he dies without a will. If your donor has no will, the laws of his state of residence will apply. And if he owns real estate outside the state of residence, these laws must also be considered. (Laws vary from state to state, but in no case is there any provision for specific charitable bequests.)

By Contract

When a husband and wife own their home jointly, title to the home goes to the survivor. A farm may also be jointly owned and at the death of one spouse the survivor gets full title to the property. As far as the farmer's home and farm are concerned, the will would not apply. These are said to have passed by contract. (While joint ownership may be just what is needed in one case, it may not be in another. Joint ownership should never be considered an adequate substitute for a will.)

Other examples of property passing outside the will by contract are: life insurance proceeds made payable to a named beneficiary; an annuity contract; various living trust arrangements; and pension and profit-sharing plans.

Planned Giving Begins with a Will

Let me illustrate how one man made use of his will to accomplish his goals for life and beyond.

Mr. Goodfriend, 73, saw an article on wills in the newsletter published by the institution I represented. He inquired for more information on wills. He was childless and had been a stroke victim and was disabled. His sister, who lived with him, had been able to carry on the farming operation through a trusted manager.

His objectives were as follows:

1. To have adequate income for as long as he or his sister lived and ample reserves to cover unforeseen emergencies.

2. To sell the property at death of the first of them, giving the trusted manager the first opportunity to buy it. The proceeds would be used to care for the survivor.

3. To give their entire estate to several charitable institutions at the death of the survivor, with the major portion going to our institution.

To accomplish these goals, first Mr. Goodfriend made a will leaving to his sister all of his personal property, which was about one-third of his total estate. If she died before he did, four specified charities would share equally in this portion of his estate.

The balance of the estate, or two-thirds of the total, valued at about $300,000, was bequeathed to the institution I represented, subject to the institution's paying his sister a fixed income through a gift annuity for as long as she lived. (The rate of payment was to be based on the gift annuity rates in effect for her age at the date of his death. The rate would be applied to the net proceeds received from the sale of the farm.)

The sister also made a will, leaving all of her personal property to her brother if living, and otherwise to the same four charities her brother had named in his will.

Because we had a wills emphasis program, we were able to help Mr. Goodfriend make plans that made the rest of his life more satisfying and provided substantial future support for my institution—support he could not have offered during his lifetime.

The Wills Emphasis Program

Here's how to begin encouraging charitable bequests. Plan a program carefully that will cover a period of at least two years. Use the following nine-point program in seeking charitable bequests for your institution.

1. Articles

First, prepare articles to be placed in your institution's magazine and newsletter. (A sample appears in Table 6.) The theme of these articles should be on the value of making a will. Show making a will as an opportunity, a privilege, and a right of every citizen.

Then prepare several articles on making bequests to charitable institutions in general and to your own institution specifically.[1]

---

[1]Remember, Mr. Goodfriend's gift was prompted by such an article.

TABLE 6
SAMPLE ARTICLE ON WILLS

YOUR OWN WILL. . . .

Because you can't assume your wishes are known.

Today, more than ever before, thoughtful people are asking themselves: "What would become of my property if I were to die suddenly?"

It may be because we have more property than ever before.

It may be because our economy seems to change more rapidly.

It may be because we need to make every provision possible for the future security of our families, as a way of completing our financial provision for them.

And almost certainly, it is because more information is available about the need for making a will and the disappointing if not tragic results when estates are settled without the help of a will.

You can know via a will

If you already have a legal will, you know what will become of your property. A person without a legal will should take note of the following:

1. *You can't just assume "my spouse gets everything."* If you have children and the husband dies first, the wife may get only a part of the estate. The state may reserve a large part for the children when they come of age, and meantime the wife may not have enough money for their proper care when she needs it.

2. *You can't just assume that estate taxes and court costs are the same with or without a will.* The simple fact is that court costs are usually higher when there is no will. Your attorney can help you include statements in your will that take full advantage of the marital deduction arrangement, for instance, and also assure that your executor can serve without bond (a cost which affects your estate).

3. *You can't just assume that because you have given generously to (name of institution) during life that a part of your estate will go to (specify work).* Even if you have told your spouse or close friends that you would like this, the court cannot, by law, take such action. Your wishes *can* be carried out if you include them in your personal will.

How to get started

To prepare your will, take the time to list all your property and assets — from house and car, to stocks, bonds, mortgages, real estate, jewelry, antiques, coin collections, and so on. Then decide what you would like to have become of these possessions when you are gone. Think in terms of the people in your life whom you would like to remember with a bequest, and of course, of those for whom you are responsible.

Remember that (name of institution) depends on the gifts and bequests of friends to accomplish its objectives both in our lifetimes and beyond.

Then, see your attorney and let him draft your will in legal form. If you need more information, just request it below.

CLIP AND MAIL TODAY

To: Planned Giving Officer
Name and Address of Institution

( ) Please send me more information on writing my will.

Name _____

Address _____

- Illustrate how a person can continue giving through his will.
- Tell the reader how to make a *final* gift to your institution through his will.
- Write about the *survivorship gift annuity* created by a person in his will.
- Through his will, a donor can provide a specific *lifetime income* for a wife, husband, child, parent, or friend and at the same time make a substantial gift to your institution. Explain how.
- Raise the question about *management problems* facing widows, who while their husbands were living were excellent managers of income but who are faced with the problem of management of principal after their husband's death. Show how well-planned wills can help solve these problems.

2. News Releases

Plan to release stories and other publicity on bequests being received. Several years ago I received the following letter from one of our client organizations:

Dear Bob:

I thought you'd like to know about a check we received in today's mail.

The executrix of an estate sent us a check for $81,567.53 as our part of the settlement of her husband's estate. The check was scribbled out just like the $20.00 checks I write at the grocery store.

Sincerely,

(Signed)

Later, the management of this mission agency contacted the executrix (female executor), who was also the widow, and worked out a story about the gift. The story told how the bequest would be used by this missionary society. It was obvious that this person had not given all of his estate to charity, because his widow was adequately and carefully provided for.

The story made it possible to establish a most valuable contact with the widow. I am sure this organization will be included when her estate is finally distributed.

The purpose of the story was to try to help readers of the organization's magazine identify with the action of this person who made his final gift through his will. Even though he is dead, he still speaks through his last gift to a needy people he had never met on the other side of the world.

3. Display Ads

Place small display-type ads in your newsletter or magazine. (See sample advertisement in Table 7.) These ads placed in house publications are probably more useful than ads placed in other publications, unless you have an adequate budget for long-time exposure in several national magazines. Or, if your donor profile indicates you have many readers of a certain magazine, then you might consider placing regular ads in that publication. For best results, go to the people who know you best.

One institution offered a free copy of a booklet about wills in a small ad in its own newsletter, which is mailed to nearly a half million people. They have received over one thousand requests for a copy of the booklet.

The amount of response will be different for each institution because the people reading the ads will differ. Older, well-established institutions should get a greater response than a new organization.

4. Brochures Mailed Quarterly

Make quarterly mailings of brochures that include a response device. These mailings are sent to the donors and ex-donors only. Don't send to your nondonor list. These brochures can be sent as a piggyback piece in another mailing, with receipts or acknowledgments, or if you prefer, send special mailings on the subject of wills. We recommend the use of the following brochures.[2]

[2]Brochures are available through Robert F. Sharpe & Co., Inc. See page 285 for further information.

TABLE 7
SAMPLE AD ON WILLS

There's A Will
in Your Future!

Is it yours—or the state's?

If you don't have a personal will when you die, state laws will take over and your estate will be distributed accordingly, in ways that you might not have chosen.

HOWEVER—

- If you have certain wishes for your estate and your heirs;
- If you would like to name your own executor, and a guardian for your minor children;
- Or, if you want to leave a bequest for (name institution) or any other worthy cause . . . you must say so in a personal will.

Before making or revising your will, be sure to see the free booklet offered here, "37 Things People 'Know' About Wills That Aren't Really So." Just use the coupon below to request it.

No obligation.

CLIP AND MAIL TODAY

To: Planned Giving Officer
    Name of institution
    Address
    City, State, Zip

Please send me a free copy of "37 Things People 'Know' About Wills That Aren't Really So." I understand there is no obligation.

NAME _____

ADDRESS _____

CITY _____

STATE _____

The first brochure mailing should be "The State Has Made Your Will." This is sent first because it has a disturbing message and will awaken interest in the minds of your donors. (See sample of letter to accompany this brochure in Table 8.)

The second quarter brochure mailing should be "When Should a Woman Write Her Will." This brochure is used to reach the women in a little more direct way. It is appropriate for male family members as well because men should be interested in encouraging the women in their lives to make wills.

The third quarter brochure mailing should be "Eleven Things to Remember If You Plan to Remember (name of your institution) In Your Will." It builds on the previous brochures and helps move the reader to action.

The fourth quarter brochure mailing should be "You Never Need to Change Your Will Unless . . ." This reminds those who already have made wills to update them regularly and to include your institution if possible.

These quarterly mailings should continue indefinitely, using additional brochures on wills and introducing other plans such as giving through life insurance, securities, and gift annuities.

5. Follow-up Mail

A carefully developed follow-up procedure is most important and absolutely necessary if you expect those who respond to your offers to include your institution in their wills.

Here is a procedure to use for those who respond to any of the above interest-getting articles, publicity, display advertisements, or brochure coupons on wills.

Initial response follow-up. If any specific questions are asked in the inquiry, answer these in the first part of your response letter. (See Table 9.) Send the booklet "37 Things People 'Know' About Wills That Aren't Really So." Explain why you are sending it and tell how the information will be of help to them. Ask them for further inquiry.

Second follow-up (thirty days later). If you have not heard from the person who received the initial response letter, send another letter, along with the booklet "Twelve Ideas from the Wills of Twelve Famous People." Tell them you think this

TABLE 8
SAMPLE LETTER TO ACCOMPANY
"THE STATE HAS MADE YOUR WILL"
(Printed letter)

Date

Dear_____,

It's not often that I speak about wills, or even think about them. But the enclosed brochure is so practical on the subject that I am prompted to share it as broadly as possible.

"The State Has Made Your Will" I hope will present two major suggestions to you: one is that your own family and loved ones will be much better able to cope with life when you are gone if you tell them and the court through your will just what you want done with your estate. A legal will is the best known way to be sure your wishes are carried out. You will save extra estate settlement expenses for your family if you have a will... but most Americans don't have one.

The other suggestion you may not have considered is including a bequest to (name of institution) in your will. This is a wonderful way to continue giving beyond your lifetime. (We have received a number of bequests in past years and all have provided needed support.) Such wills are a tremendous inspiration to others.

If this subject interests you, I hope you will ask for our little booklet, "37 Things People 'Know' About Wills That Aren't Really So." This is an eye-opening few minutes of reading that can benefit you and your loved ones. Use the enclosed card to request your copy.

Sincerely,

second booklet may provide additional helpful ideas and that you believe reading it will benefit them. Ask for further inquiry.

Third follow-up (60 days after initial response follow-up). Assuming you have not heard from the inquirer, send another letter and enclose "Giving Through Your Will." Tell how to use this booklet. Suggest the person study it carefully, complete the forms in the booklet, and take it to his or her own attorney for drafting the will—putting personal wishes in legal form. In-

TABLE 9
SAMPLE LETTER TO ACCOMPANY
"37 THINGS PEOPLE 'KNOW' ABOUT WILLS
THAT AREN'T REALLY SO"
(Personally typed letter)

Date

Type in Name
Address
City, State, Zip

Dear Mr. and Mrs._____,

Here is your copy of our wills booklet, "37 Things People 'Know' About Wills That Aren't Really So." I'm glad you requested it because I believe you will find it helpful.

Many of our friends are taking a new look at their financial plans as a result of our current emphasis on will-making. It's a good excuse to review goals and dreams with and for our families, and to see if these goals are realistic and in keeping with our highest commitments.

If you haven't written your will yet, you will find in this booklet many reasons why you should. If you <u>have</u> written it, you will find suggestions for reviewing it and perhaps amending it to include new items.

Either way, do remember the possibilities of a charitable bequest in your will. Many people find great satisfaction in leaving a specific amount or a percentage of their estates to the cause or causes they supported regularly during their lifetimes.

If you have any questions about wills—or about any other giving plans or possibilities—feel free to write or phone me about them. I'll be glad to help in any way possible.

Sincerely,

P. S. Remember that bequests can also be designated as memorial gifts to honor the memory of parents, beloved teachers, or others whose lives added meaning to your own.

clude in this letter several suggested forms of bequests for use by the attorncy.

This response procedure is based on the assumption that few will inquire quickly. But, whenever someone indicates that he is taking action on making his will, pull his name out of this procedure and follow-up personally as soon as possible with a telephone call or a personal visit—or both.

6. Personal Contact

Making personal contact with those who respond is of utmost importance in securing charitable bequests. What we have suggested doing up to this point is to try to get a few people in your constituency to "raise their hands," that is, to identify themselves as persons who may have some interest in making wills, revising their wills, or even including your institution in their wills.

In our seminars we are often asked, "how do you get before the people and actually 'close the sale'?"

We have learned from experience that some people will make their wills naming your institution as beneficiary by the mail process alone. We also know this is not the usual case.

Once you have received an inquiry and followed it up by mail, we recommend you write a special letter or make a telephone call offering to visit this person. For example, you can plan a trip to a particular area and advise all the inquirers in that area by letter that you will be there during a certain period. Tell them you plan to call them while you are there to see if a visit is practical at that time. Some of these people will see you.

From this visit you will probably be able to plan some action: Either eliminate this inquirer from your list or turn him into a first-rate prospect for a bequest or some other type of current or deferred gift. Remember, it is important to keep cleaning your files. Don't keep the names of people who have no interest in your institution in your files.

We have been asked many times if it is better to telephone the prospect or just walk in on him. There are institutions following both practices successfully. In our opinion, people resent a

111

knock on the door as the initial approach. We believe it is best to telephone the person and ask for an appointment, telling exactly why you want a personal interview. Many prospects have expressed to us their appreciation for our taking the appointment approach. They also have told us how much they dislike the "drop in" or the "I just happened to be in your area" approach.

It is important to learn to work with the lawyers of these prospects. It is also advisable to have your institution's attorney work with the prospect's attorney. Some institutions make a practice of providing an attorney for drawing up wills for their donors. It is obvious that this approach appeals to some donors. We do not advise this kind of practice, however, because each person should have his will drawn up by his own trusted attorney who is up-to-date on local state laws.

We suggest that you have a list of several attorneys from which the prospect might select counsel if he has no attorney of his own.

7. Follow-up Visits

Follow-up interviews with persons you know have included your institution in their wills can prove of great value. With a periodic contact, you establish confidence and these persons often open up and tell you much more about themselves and their property. The wide-awake representative will recognize new gift opportunities and advise the donor of them. He may be able to start a series of current gifts of securities or help them arrange gift annuities, trusts, and life insurance. Eventually, he may assist them as they plan ahead, naming your institution for a much larger part of their estates.

8. Getting Bequest Information

"How can we find out who has included us in their wills?" is a question often asked by planned giving officers.

Many people are eager to tell you, and they will without any effort on your part. Others won't tell you and don't want you to know. Some people will resent a direct question.

What we have done, without any known resentment, is to

add a sentence on a response coupon that appears to be an afterthought, with a box for checking. The sentence reads:

☐ I have already included (name of institution) in my will.

Some planned giving officers make a great effort to find out if their institution has been included in their donors' wills. They even push to find out the amount of the bequest. This practice has been known to cost an institution the bequest. Management often encourages this practice indirectly by putting pressure on the planned giving officer to show results, and he then goes too far in trying to get information.

I personally have little confidence in production reports that include a substantial amount of potential bequests that will come to an institution. We are better off not knowing these amounts unless they are freely revealed.

9. Receiving the Bequest

The final step in this program is receiving the bequest. You will learn in one of several ways that your institution is included in a person's will. You will usually be notified by the executor or you may first learn of it through a publication.

Once you know who the executor is, you should advise him or her that your institution is a tax-exempt institution (for federal tax purposes) and that you are exempt from state inheritance and estate taxes. An investigation should be made to determine if your institution is exempt from state death taxes in the state where the deceased person had lived. You should also ask for a copy of the will, offering to pay duplication and mailing expenses.

In six months, if you haven't had further notice, write to the executor. When a year has passed, ask your attorney to make inquiry.

Let's **summarize** these nine points:

1. Prepare articles on wills to be included in your institution's magazine or newsletter.

2. Release stories and other publicity on bequests received by your institution.

3. Place small display ads on wills in your institution's magazine or newsletter.

4. Make quarterly mailings of brochures on wills and other deferred giving subjects.

5. Develop a thorough follow-up procedure on inquiries.

6. Make telephone and personal calls to those showing more interest.

7. Follow up periodically and look for larger giving opportunities for the prospect.

8. Don't use too much pressure to find out who has included you in their wills.

9. When notified of a pending bequest, follow through thoroughly.

Five Ways to Include
A Charitable Bequest

There are five effective ways your donors can include your institution in their wills, depending on their own plans and situations:

1. Ask the person to include your institution for a specific amount.

2. Ask the person to include your institution for a percent of the estate.

3. Ask the person to include your institution for the residue of the estate. (Most people, once they have made specific distributions, put a residuary clause in their wills and designate other beneficiaries or charitable institutions to receive the residuary.)

4. Ask the person to include your institution for a specific amount or a percent of the estate plus a part or all of the residue.

5. Ask the person to provide an income for a loved one through the will by establishing a survivorship annuity or some type of charitable remainder trust. You can also have the bequest designated for general purposes, a memorial, and/or an endowment.

Reminders for Will-Makers

When a person has decided to draft a will, there are a number of things he should include:

1. Name an executor. The executor is the individual who will be responsible for settling the estate. This includes collecting the assets of the estate, paying all of the last debts and expenses, paying all taxes that might be due, and finally making the distribution of the assets according to the terms of the will. In the event an executor is not named in the will, it becomes the responsibility of the probate court to name an administrator who will have the same functions.

It is obviously better to name an executor or executrix whom you are close to and who you know will exercise his or her duties conscientiously. A will may preclude the executor from having to post bond with the probate court. In cases of intestacy, a bond must be filed and this is usually an unnecessary expense of the estate.

2. When there are minor children to be considered in an estate plan, guardians should be named in the will. This should be done in order to insure that the children will be cared for by somebody who is willing and responsible in case of the death of the testator. This provision particularly needs to cover the possibility of there being no surviving spouse, in case the two should die in a common disaster. A failure to name a guardian in the will once again places the responsibility on the probate court to make these appointments.

3. Common disaster provisions are usually included in a will to insure that property will pass from the estate of the husband to the wife, and vice-versa, before passing to the ultimate beneficiaries. In this way, both estates will qualify for the marital deduction. Otherwise, most state laws provide that each estate will pass directly to heirs without going through the surviving spouse's estate, thus *not* qualifying for the marital deduction. The common disaster clause will also insure that the property in these cases would pass according to the wishes of the testator and not according to the state

115

laws of descent and distribution. Check local state laws. This is where you might be of considerable help to your prospect.

4. A provision should be made for the marital deduction if the testator wants to care for his or her spouse and enjoy the full tax advantage of estate planning; not having a will or including the marital deduction provision in the will might cause some unnecessary taxes. The marital deduction is a federal law. Some state laws have a comparable marital deduction statute for inheritance taxes, but most states have other exemptions that need to be checked. The type of property that is going to be used to fulfill the marital deduction might also be spelled out in the marital clause.

Let me point out here that it is not necessary to have a will in order to take advantage of the marital deduction, but because of the peculiarity of state laws, it is best to have it spelled out to insure that the wife or husband gets up to one-half of the estate, and thus the property qualifies.

5. The testator might be wise to designate certain properties or monies from which the last debts and expenses and the taxes should be paid. This clause would be used to prevent an unnecessary sale of a particular parcel of real estate or perhaps a part of the business. Life insurance has solved *many* of these liquidity problems because it represents a cash distribution to the estate or one of the beneficiaries at the death of the testator.

6. A residuary clause should always be a part of the will. This clause will insure that anything not specifically bequeathed or devised will pass in a manner consistent with the testator's wishes. This particular clause can also take into account any increased assets that the estate might experience. This should never be the substitute for the reviewing of a will, however.

Between Drafting and Probating

Between drafting and probate, the most important thing that an individual can do about his will is to keep it up-to-date, reviewing it carefully at least once every year. Wills should be reviewed even more often than that when some particular circumstance takes place calling for a change in the will, such as a move to another state or the death of a beneficiary, executor, or guardian, or in case there has been a substantial increase or decline in the assets of an estate.

Along these lines I recall the story of a man who wrote his will in 1948 leaving to his wife a specific $20,000 bequest. He specifically bequeathed $3,000 to each of the children, and then left the residue and remainder of his estate to their house-keeper. At the time this was a very modest sum of $250. The man deposited his will in his lockbox and never removed it. He never studied it and never had it redrawn.

He died in 1963, fifteen years later, and according to the terms of the will, the executor was to make a distribution of $20,000 to his wife, $3,000 to each of his children, and the residue of $88,000 to his housekeeper. Even though the wife dissented the will, she was still only entitled to a lesser share under state law than the husband would have certainly wanted her to have.

This is just one example of why it is important to keep a will properly updated. This man's assets had greatly increased and even though there were no changes with respect to the bene-ficiaries, the amount of money each received was quite differ-ent from what the testator would have wanted them to receive.

We have tried to explore some of the things that can happen between drafting and probating a will. Understanding these concepts as a planned giving officer will help you in working with your potential donors so that you in turn can render a service to them. Remember, since none of the state laws of descent and distribution makes provision for direct charitable bequests, you must "educate" your donors to plan such final gifts through a legal will. Only in this way will your institution have a chance to benefit.

This can be successfully accomplished by the use of direct mail and also through wills clinics where you assemble a small group of your donors to inform them of the effects of having a valid will and the disastrous effects of not having one.

A Wills Clinic Program

Here is a brief outline for a wills clinic program:

Preparation

1. Make a list of people—ten or more who share a common interest in the church, college (alumni group), hospital, youth work, or other charitable cause you represent.

2. Send an invitation to the clinic and a copy of the brochure "The State Has Made Your Will" and ask them to reserve a place by returning an enclosed card.

3. Ask a leader of the group (probably a donor already) to serve as host, in his home if the group is small, at another meeting place if the group is large.

4. Invite one or two lawyers who (if possible) are known to the group. The lawyers, the representative of your organization, and the host will participate in the panel discussion during the program.

Program

1. Introduction—five minutes. The *host* tells the purpose of the meeting and introduces each panelist. (The purpose of the meeting is to gain information about the benefits, legal aspects, and the giving opportunities of making a will. The host explains that will-making is something that more than half of our adult population is neglecting to the disadvantage of their own families and the worthy causes they believe in.)

2. Slide/Film presentation, "The State Has Made Your Will"—twelve minutes. The *representative* of the organization will show the production or will have appointed someone who is familiar with the machines and can set them up ahead of time.

3. Summary and suggestions from the representative: Why Don't People Make Wills?—five minutes. The *representative* may suggest these answers:

- They are reluctant to face death.
- They think they own an insignificant amount of property.
- They think wills are too expensive.

118

- They don't know how to start.
- They procrastinate.
- They hold all property jointly.

4. Panel discussion—twenty-eight minutes. The leader of the panel (host or representative of the organization) should repeat all questions. Each attorney should be asked at least one of these questions:

- What happens to property *in this state* if a person dies without a will?
- Who decides what happens to minor children when parents are killed simultaneously? What happens to property if there are no children?

5. "Ways to Include a Charity in Your Will"—five minutes. The representative briefly lists the five basic bequest possibilities:

- Name the charity for a *specific amount*.
- Name the charity for a *percent* of the estate.
- Name the charity for the *residue* (what is left after other bequests are made).
- Name the charity for a specific amount or a percent of the estate *plus* a part or all of the residue.
- Leave a guaranteed *fixed life income* to a loved one through your will, with the charity receiving the residue (a survivorship gift annuity).

The representative offers his time and services to anyone wanting to talk further about giving through his will.

6. Conclusion—five minutes. The *host* thanks everyone for coming. He offers free literature and may end with comments summarizing these points:

> We *work* to earn money.
> We *struggle* to save money.
> We *learn* to give money.
> And it's just as important that we know how to *leave* money!

It is a good idea at this point to have refreshments available so that those who are interested can meet the participants and ask questions in private conversation. Free materials on wills can be made available on the table in the area where the refreshments are being served.

Follow-Up

A week after the clinic, the representative may write a letter to each person who attended, enclosing a copy of "37 Things People Know About Wills That Aren't Really So."

Chapter Ten
The Ways People
Give—Later
Part 2: Life Insurance

Basic to the whole matter of giving is man's built-in need to give. Somehow we have the mistaken idea that as financial development workers we are in effect trying to talk people into doing something they really don't want to do—that is, give.

But this isn't true; man has a need to give. He wants to do something permanent. As one person said, "Man wants to 'outlive' his own death." He enjoys seeing his name perpetuated.

When people want to give and are motivated to give but are financially unable to give an amount that they feel is personally significant, there is a vehicle that will allow them to make a purposeful, useful charitable gift: It is through the means of *life insurance*.

Big Business

Life insurance is one of the top ten industries in America. At the end of 1976 the *Life Insurance Fact Book* (1977 edition) reported $2.34 trillion worth of life insurance in force. Death benefits paid to policyholders in 1976 totaled $9.6 billion, while living benefits to policyholders amounted to $15 billion.

Basically, a life insurance policy is a contract issued by a life insurance company to an individual. The life insurance company agrees to pay a fixed amount of money after a certain number of years or at death, for a consideration of a predetermined premium, payable over a definite period of years or for the life of the policyholder.

Ninety-five percent of American families own life insurance. The average amount of life insurance on all families in the United States is $30,100. This is equal to a little more than two times the disposable personal income per family.

Stated in its simplest terms, life insurance is money! It represents one of the largest untapped resources for charitable institutions today.

The life expectancy for males in this country is 67 years and for females 74.3 years. These statistics show us why so many of our deferred giving donors are women. Wives often live to inherit their husbands' estates and are more able to make final substantial gifts to charitable institutions.

Life insurance agents can be cultivated and motivated to sell charitable life insurance, and I believe charities should do everything possible to involve agents from all life insurance companies in selling charitable life insurance.

The case of Mrs. Mary North, age 65, is a good example. Her husband died four years ago at age 63. He left his entire estate to her. During their life together, they never gave much thought to giving away any of their estate at death. Mr. and Mrs. North jointly owned a family business. They had purchased $50,000 of life insurance on each of them to provide cash to help the survivor keep the business going. A year after his death, she sold the business but retained the life insurance policy on her life. She learned the policy had $32,000 of cash value. At age 65, she stopped paying premiums of $1,400 a year and surrendered the policy for cash.

The money from the policy was placed in a gift annuity with a charitable organization, and she received payments of nearly $2,000 a year for life, most of which was free from income taxes. While she gave up $50,000 of life insurance she no longer needed, she increased her annual spendable income by nearly $3,400. She saved the $1,400 premium and received $2,000 payment from a gift annuity.

Since there were no children she was free to make a substantial gift and at the same time increase her own income. All she did was exchange an unneeded, non-income-producing asset for a plan that produced more disposable income.

It is true she could have received more income from a commercial life insurance company annuity, but she chose the charitable gift annuity because she wanted to give to the institution.

Eight Advantages of Giving Life Insurance

1. A Life Insurance Gift Is Certain

The proceeds are payable immediately at maturity or at death in cash. The policy is not subject to probate costs or delays in the settlement of the estate if paid to a named beneficiary other than the estate.

2. A Life Insurance Gift Is Complete

The institution receives all the proceeds. Because life insurance bypasses probate, and the laws exempt charitable gifts from usual estate taxes, it arrives intact. A $10,000 life insurance policy is received as $10,000, whereas a $10,000 bequest may be reduced by fees to $9,000 by the time it is received.

3. A Life Insurance Gift Is Easier to Make

A donor pays for life insurance in small, regular amounts (annual premiums). This makes easier accumulation of a larger-than-average charitable gift. In effect the total gift is created when the policy is written, and it is paid for over the years.

4. A Life Insurance Gift Is Personal

A donor can plan, arrange, and announce his gift himself, and he knows it will occur just as planned.

5. A Life Insurance Gift Is Thoughtful of Heirs

The donor's estate is not diminished, because life insurance, by its very nature, creates what amounts to an additional, separate "estate." Few heirs take exception to life insurance "bequests."

6. A Life Insurance Gift Is Discreet

A life insurance policy is not a matter of public record, therefore not subject to the publicity that sometimes accompanies estate settlements.

7. A Life Insurance Gift Is Economical

Frequently, under certain circumstances, the size of a person's final gift is actually larger than the original cost. The premiums are deductible on federal income tax returns when the irrevocable owner and beneficiary is a qualified charitable institution.

8. A Life Insurance Gift Is Convenient

Many potential donors already own "used" policies—policies that have finished serving their original purposes and are now available for your institution. And changing the beneficiaries on a policy is much simpler than setting up a trust, making a will, or arranging other forms of deferred giving.

Basic Plans

It is important for the planned giving officer to understand the basics of how life insurance policies can be arranged to provide gifts to his institution.

When he is interviewing a prospective donor he should be able to discuss life insurance plans and recognize the opportunities for charitable giving through life insurance.

The basic plans of life insurance are listed below.

Ordinary Life

This type may be referred to as straight life or whole life. The life insurance company charges a level premium for the life of the policy holder. This is the best known life insurance policy and the policy that is most often purchased.

Limited Payment Life

This is a policy with a higher level premium that is paid for a limited number of years, such as five, ten, fifteen, twenty, twenty-five, or thirty years.

Retirement Income

This type provides a small amount of life insurance protection at death but a large amount of cash value at retirement time. (The purpose of this policy is to provide a fixed life income for the insured person in the amount of $10 per month per $1,000 of original insurance. Premiums are paid from the time the policy commences until the retirement.)

Endowment

These policies are written for various terms of years. The premiums are paid for a specified term. If the policyholder dies during the term, the face amount of the policy is paid to the beneficiary. If he lives until the end of the term, the face amount of the policy is paid to the policyholder.

Term Life

This plan is written for a period of years, ranging from one year to age 65 or 70, or even age 100. The initial term life premiums are much lower than ordinary life and the other policies previously mentioned.

Minimum Deposit Life

This is an ordinary life policy for which the owner borrows the money from the new policy to help pay the premiums. When he dies, the loan is deducted from the policy proceeds. This arrangement is, in effect, a decreasing term policy.

Reduced to simplest terms, there are basically just two kinds of life insurance policies given as charitable gifts: (1) existing policies, and (2) new policies.

Within these categories are a variety of plans from which your institution could benefit.

Six Ways of Giving Existing Policies

1. Your donor might name your institution as primary beneficiary of a retirement type policy in case he or she does not live to retirement.

2. Your donor might name the institution for a share of the insurance, perhaps a percent. If a person regularly gives a

certain percent of his income while he lives, he is likely to give the same percent at death.

3. A donor can name your institution as the secondary beneficiary.

4. A policyholder can name your institution as the *final beneficiary* after all other beneficiaries have been satisfied.

5. A donor can name your institution as the residual beneficiary on a retirement type policy before he or she starts receiving lifetime payments.

Suppose Mrs. Monroe has a $20,000 death benefit and is 65 years old. She has the option of electing a life income of approximately $150 a month, but if she dies in two years, the life insurance company keeps the balance of the $20,000.

She could, instead, elect a life and ten-year certain option and guarantee an income of approximately $130 to $140 a month for life. If she dies in two years, the $130 to $140 a month will be paid to your institution for eight more years. This could be a windfall. No understanding donor wants a life insurance company to get his hard-earned money when it could be given to your institution. For a surprisingly small sacrifice of monthly income, a donor may make a substantial gift.($140 a month for eight years is $13,440. This could be what your institution would receive if the donor died at age 67.)

6. A donor may name your institution to receive the policy dividends by assignment. Policy dividends are *not* reportable as income and *are* deductible as gifts.

As simple and fundamental as it may seem, most of us would never consider these six easy methods of encouraging donors to give to our charitable, religious, or educational institutions through life insurance policies they now own. And yet, all of us would agree that *we are talking here about a relatively untapped source of dollars* that are available to underwrite the goals and dreams that our institutions are seeking to attain in the near and distant future.

Ways of Giving New Policies

It is advisable to encourage your donors to purchase new life insurance policies:

- To guarantee or replace charitable bequests.
- To replace for family heirs the funds transferred as an outright gift or life income gift.
- To guarantee substantial pledges.
- To increase a donor's gift.
- To endow annual giving.
- To solve special problems.

(Closed corporation stockholders can be encouraged to purchase life insurance on their own lives, naming your institution as beneficiary.)

Life Insurance Ideas That Work

Here are some examples of how these types of gifts work to help the giver accomplish his goals for supporting your institution.

Guarantee a Bequest Through Life Insurance

One donor wanted to include a $10,000 bequest to an institution in his will. His insurance agent showed him how, instead, he could purchase a $10,000 life insurance policy on the ordinary life plan, guarantee his gift, and get the benefit of federal income tax deductions equal to the annual premiums while he lives. Premiums are deductible when a qualified institution is the irrevocable owner and beneficiary.

Replacing Gifts with Life Insurance

I have a friend who owned stock in one of the well-known growth companies. His $20,000 investment had grown to almost $200,000. But he was "stock poor," because he had come to the place in life where he needed more income. The dividend of less than one percent just wasn't doing the job for him. He had so much capital appreciation he didn't want to sell the stocks and pay the capital gains tax.

My friend had a strong giving motive and was interested in a small college. He transferred $50,000 of this stock to the college as a gift to its pooled income fund. At current interest rates, the fund is returning him 6 percent. At his age, 50, a substantial

127

income tax deduction is allowed. All capital gains taxes are avoided.

My friend's annual income is increased from $400 in stock dividends to about $3,000 a year, but he reduces his assets by $50,000. He was able to overcome his concern about reducing the size of his estate by having his wife purchase $50,000 of ordinary life insurance on his life. She owns the policy, pays the premiums from her own personal resources, and is named the beneficiary. The proceeds from this policy will not be taxed in his estate at the time of death but will pass directly to his wife.

The increased income from the life income arrangement is sufficient to pay the new premiums and it has helped him to diversify his investments and assure himself of a basic retirement program. But more important, my friend made a substantial gift to the college, something he had wanted to do for a long time.

Guaranteeing a Pledge

One donor made a pledge of $500 a month for ten years to an institution. The charity realized it would lose much if this gift did not materialize. The institution asked the donor to consider purchasing $60,000 worth of ten-year reducing term insurance to guarantee the payment of this pledge if he died. The donor agreed and the premium paid by the donor was deductible on his federal income tax return as a gift.

Double or Triple Your Gift Through Life Insurance

Sometimes couples in their forties will transfer $10,000, $15,000, or $20,000 to a favorite charitable institution in a small revocable living trust. Some people are attracted to the idea of including a provision in the trust permitting the trustee to purchase a life insurance policy on the life of the trustor, naming the institution as the irrevocable beneficiary.

Here is how it works: The trustee purchases the life insurance policy and pays the premium. The institution is the irrevocable owner and beneficiary. It is possible to purchase a joint life insurance policy that pays the full face amount on the death of the first to die. This makes possible a gift while a survivor lives, as well as the original trust gift at death.

These donors can double the gift they made through a revocable living trust and life insurance. In fact, they can triple the gift by continuing the joint life insurance policy on the life of the survivor of them. This option is available in joint life policies issued by some life insurance companies.

Endowing the Donor's Gift

A certain donor had been giving $5,000 a year for the past eight years to a particular charity. When he learned it takes four to five new donors to replace a donor who dies, it was possible to persuade him to endow his annual gifts for a period of five years to give the charity time to recruit the new donors. He did this by purchasing $25,000 worth of ordinary life insurance naming the institution as the irrevocable owner and beneficiary. The premiums were deductible. After his death, the life insurance company will pay the institution $5,000 a year plus interest for five years.

Take Care of Heirs Using Life Insurance

Another person wanted to provide $15,000 for each of his three children from his substantial estate. By placing his entire estate in a revocable living trust, he was able to give his estate to certain charitable institutions and provide for his children at the same time. It was arranged for the trust to purchase $45,000 of life insurance on the donor's life, pay the premiums, and name the children as beneficiaries for $15,000 each. Through life insurance, he was able to provide for his children without disturbing the trust principal or other assets.

These seven plans are ideas that work. They work, not because they are schemes, but because they solve a particular need or problem of a person motivated to give.

Let the Corporation Pay the Premiums

Ask members of your board of trustees or other donors who are presidents of closely held family corporations to have their corporations purchase charitable life insurance on their own lives, naming your institution as the irrevocable owner and beneficiary. The premiums are tax deductible to the corporation. Charitable deductions are limited to 5 percent of the corporation's taxable income.

Now let's turn our attention to setting up a program for your institution to attract gifts of life insurance. The following is a plan which can work for you.

Ideal Charitable Life Insurance Program

First, list the names and business addresses of selected life underwriters in your high constituency areas. The names can probably be obtained from the local life underwriters' associations. The selection of names for your list should include leading men and women representing all kinds of companies and agencies without regard to their relationship to your institution. The goal is to be in touch with the agents who are most likely handling the life insurance needs of your donors.

The life insurance agent is in a position to help you. He is in touch with many of your donors and since he is compensated with sales commissions, you can secure his competent help without cost.

Second, list the names and addresses of donors and others you believe should be included in mailings promoting life insurance gifts. List donors of all ages. Don't forget people who are in their early twenties. Many of these younger donors can give more *only* through life insurance.

Your young donor is already buying most of the important things in his life on time payments—his home, auto, personal life insurance, and so on. He is already familiar with the idea of time payments. It is part of his everyday life, so why shouldn't he do the same with a gift to your institution? All he has to do to make a gift of $10,000 is take out a life insurance policy and then make the payments of about $15 a month as they come due.

Third, prepare a series of mailings to each name on the list and continue these mailings at least once a year for several years.

- Send a simple brochure on ways to give life insurance. The brochure should include a response device offering additional information about giving life insurance. Those who respond are sent another letter with the material requested. The prospect should be advised to discuss charitable life insurance with his own agent, or if he prefers he can write to you.
- Send a letter to the insurance agents (see sample in Table 10) on your list and enclose a copy of the brochure you mailed to your prospect list, as well as a copy of the follow-up booklet you are sending to the persons asking for more information. Periodically send letters and case studies to the agents.

Fourth, prepare a series of articles and ads to be placed in your "house organ" to reach the masses on your mailing list. It would also be helpful to send copies to the list of underwriters. Be sure to include a coupon at the end of each article or ad so the reader can easily respond.

Fifth, when you have a high concentration of donors and agents in a given area, plan several seminars on charitable life insurance for one to three hours at a time. Invite agents and selected donors to participate. A college or university could set up such a seminar on campus. A denomination could have such a meeting in a leading church and invite people to attend from local sister churches.

Sixth, arrange a joint meeting with the local life underwriters association and executives of all the local charities. The program (perhaps a luncheon) should include ideas on how the two groups can cooperate. A ten-minute presentation by a person from each group and a twenty-minute panel discussion session would make a good program.

When you start receiving inquiries, your staff must be able to work with the agent of the donor's choice in arranging existing or new life insurance to solve the inquirer's problems and accomplish his goals.

When soliciting life insurance gifts remember to

131

TABLE 10
SAMPLE LETTER TO LIFE UNDERWRITERS

Dear _____,

As a life underwriter who is also acquainted with (INSTITUTION NAME), you may find the enclosed information of surprising interest.

I am sending a brochure and a booklet on ways to use life insurance for more effective giving to charitable institutions such as ours. Also, there is a booklet giving background on (INSTITUTION NAME), and a file folder to keep this information in. In the future, I will be sending you some actual case histories that may be of interest to you.

Please give particular attention to the life insurance booklet. I would appreciate knowing your reaction to it. Let me know if you can use additional copies for some of your clients, prospects or fellow life underwriters. It is intended to be helpful to them as well as to us. Many people don't realize how easily and generously they can give through life insurance.

And many life underwriters, as you well know, seldom stop to think that a man's charitable giving interests can often turn him from a poor insurance prospect into a good one. This is especially true of three types of "problem prospects":

- The man who has "enough insurance." If he's really that well off, he's an excellent prospect for a life insurance policy to give to a favored institution.

- The man who needs no protection. If his responsibilities to relatives are really completed, he should be able to give to a worthy cause and may want to protect or replace his gift with insurance.

- The man over 50. It's usually late for him to buy more life insurance to protect his growing family, but a prime time to consider charitable giving and the life insurance that it may involve.

Do you want additional copies of these booklets? I'll be glad to send you as many as you can use.

Sincerely yours,

Planned Giving Officer

132

— refuse requests for a list of your good donors. Don't give or sell such a list to any agent or company.

— develop a program to include all agents and companies in your constituency area. The life insurance gift promotion should be paid for by the nonprofit institution. Don't expect life insurance companies to pay the bills.

— establish seminars on charitable life insurance in high-interest locations for local agents and selected donors.

— provide adequate information to your constituency about ways to give life insurance. Advise your interested prospect to see his own agent or write to your institution. *Do not recommend any agent or company. Recommend that the donor use his own agent.*

— do not contact small donors with the idea of putting a few dollars into a small insurance policy for your institution *instead* of making a gift. This approach is unsatisfactory for everyone because needed current gifts will be used to pay premiums.

Conclusion

The suggestion to give life insurance must come from you. If you wait for the prospective donor to suggest its use, the chances are almost zero that your institution will ever receive any gifts from this important source.

One of the biggest problems in using life insurance for charitable purposes lies in the mind of the planned giving officer himself. He tends to consider life insurance as something "different" or "special" and feels that because he doesn't know a great deal about the subject, it is best to avoid it completely.

(However, if you were to follow this line of reasoning, then you would not ask a donor to remember your institution in his will simply because you aren't a lawyer.)

You don't have to be an expert to know that life insurance can be a valuable vehicle of giving for your donor and your institution. The donor's life insurance agent can handle all the technical matters when you and the donor explain to the agent just what it is you're trying to accomplish.

Life insurance has a big advantage over other kinds of property. A person creates his estate and then gives it. From the time he pays the first premium for his life insurance policy, he already owns the amount he ultimately wants to give.

Chapter Eleven
The Ways People
Give—Now *and* Later
Part I: Gift Annuities

Every charitable institution receives current gifts, the *now* income that helps keep it in business day by day.

A growing number of these also have a deferred giving program. Their donors are planning ahead with the institution in mind by including the institution in their wills and life insurance.

But comparatively few charitable institution managers are realizing their fair share of the now *and* later type gifts we are discussing in this chapter. Some believe these gifts are too sophisticated for their donors.

I understand the problems involved. I also know that a properly managed institution can incorporate these giving-for-income plans to significant advantage and welcome a host of new donors whose help is needed by the institution, and who need help in planning their own financial future.

In this chapter we'll discuss charitable gift annuities; in the next chapter we'll consider annuity trusts, unitrusts, and the pooled income fund.

We will emphasize how securities can be used to the donor's advantage in funding any of these plans. Many of your best prospects will be stock owners who are not satisfied with what their investments are accomplishing—either for themselves or for their favorite charitable institutions.

Gift Annuities—Charitable Give and Take

A charitable gift annuity is an agreement by which a donor is able to make a gift of money or other property to a qualified charitable institution conditioned on the institution's making guaranteed annual stipulated payments for the life or lives of one or two persons. The institution issuing charitable gift annuity agreements must be a *qualified charity*. In other words, it should be a tax-exempt public charity and have investment "know how" before receiving the donor's funds or making annual payments. (Check with your own tax advisors to determine the limit your annuitants can deduct as a charitable gift.) Some states require a permit to offer charitable gift annuities to residents of the state.

Qualified charities are listed in the cumulative list provided by the U. S. Treasury Department, Internal Revenue Service, publication number 78. A qualified institution that is not listed should make an effort to see that its name is listed. If both a corporate name and a trade name are in use, it is wise to seek a dual listing in the cumulative list.

Guaranteed stipulated payments are based on the age of the donor and, of course, the amount of the gift. The annuity can be so arranged that the annual payments will be made for the life of the person acquiring the annuity and/or for the life of a surviving person. The minimum amount should be no less than $500. Some institutions make $1,000 or $2,500 the minimum.

Types of Gift Annuities

There are four basic types of gift annuities:

1. *Single life gift annuities* are based on the life of one person.

2. *Joint and survivorship gift annuities* are based on the lives of two persons. The gift is provided by both parties. Payments are made to both persons for life, then to the survivor.

3. *Survivorship gift annuities* may be arranged during the person's lifetime or created by a will or trust. By this plan, payment is made to the giver for life, then to his designated

survivor for the rest of his/her life. A substantial gift is delivered to the charitable institution at death of the survivor.

4. *Deferred payment gift annuities* are arranged now, but payments begin at a later time at a higher rate than would be paid now. These gift annuities may be based on either one or two lives.

Terminology is very important. What the donor receives from the charity is referred to as an *annual payment*. It is not interest or dividends. The *deductible amount* for federal income tax purposes is known as the gift portion. The *actuarial cost* is the amount of money plus interest needed to be invested now to guarantee the future annual payments. This approximates the cost of a commercial life insurance company annuity that would yield about the same amount of annual payment. The *expected return* is the total amount of payments the annuitant(s) is expected to receive during lifetime. The *exclusion ratio* is the part of the annual payments excluded from the donor's federal income tax return.

What Schedule of Rates Should You Use?

The Committee on Gift Annuities (an organization established and supported by charitable institutions issuing gift annuities), among other things, makes actuarial studies to determine what rates are to be offered. These rates are the same for both male and female annuitants. The rates have been computed to produce, on the average, a "residuum" or *gift* to the institution at death of the annuitants of approximately 50 percent of the amount originally given for the agreement.

If your institution uses higher rates, there will be a smaller gift portion, and a lower income tax deduction. While actuaries may be employed to develop your own schedule of rates, I suggest using the rates recommended by the Committee on Gift Annuities. (The address is Committee on Gift Annuities, 1875 Broadway, New York, New York 10023.)

The following are examples of the Committee on Gift Annuities' recommended annual payments at various ages. These rates were effective May, 1980.

Age	Annual payment to be paid to annuitants
60	6.2%
65	6.5%
70	7.1%
75	7.9%
80	9.2%
90 and over	14.0%

Joint and survivorship rates are lower than single life rates. Actuaries have determined that the institution incurs a greater liability when making payments to a couple, even though the age of the youngest of the two persons may be the same as a single person giving for a charitable gift annuity.

EXAMPLES: For a couple whose ages are 60 and 65, the joint rate is 5.9 percent ($59 per thousand), compared to 6.2 percent for an individual age 60. For a couple whose ages are 80 and 85, the joint rate would be 8.9 percent compared to 9.2 percent for an individual age 80.

In my experience, I have found the rate differences sometimes create unfortunate competition. Since a gift annuity is not generally considered a good investment, an alert institution seeks to secure annuity gifts from people who have *a strong donative intent*, not from those seeking a high return on their investment. If a person is looking for a higher return, he can get higher payments from annuities issued by life insurance companies and from many bonds. The rate schedule is selected by the issuing institution and should be approved by a qualified actuary.

Donor's Benefits

Just what are the benefits of a charitable gift annuity for the donor?

1. He makes a gift to the institution of his choice.
2. He secures fixed annual payments for life.
3. He is relieved of money management concerns.

4. He gets certain tax benefits because there is an irrevocable gift, and part of the annual payments represent return of his principal.

Institution's Benefits

1. Public relations values multiply to the institution as it provides the donor a service—a way to give and yet receive an income for life. Often the donor's friends also become gift annuitants.

2. The institution receives a substantial portion of the initial amount placed in the annuity as a gift.

3. Regular contact is established with the donor, making possible further cultivation for other types of gifts.

What About Taxes?

Here is a brief summary of the tax considerations affecting gift annuities as of January 1, 1978.

Federal Income Tax

- The donor is allowed an income tax deduction when he gives for a gift annuity . . . usually about one-third of the amount placed in the gift annuity.
- The donor can prorate any capital gains tax due when appreciated property is exchanged for a charitable gift annuity, because realized capital gains are spread over the life expectancy of the annuitant.
- The annuitant receives guaranteed annual payments that are largely tax free.

State Income Tax

State laws are also applicable. Check Chapter 17 and Appendix 2 for information on state laws and federal estate taxes.

Using Securities to Fund Gift Annuities

Let's emphasize here the importance of using appreciated securities to fund a charitable gift annuity contract.

EXAMPLE: Mrs. Sarah Gregory, age 72, gives appreciated stocks to her favorite charitable institution to fund a gift annuity of $10,000. She purchased the stocks eight years ago for less than the value now. She will have a reportable capital gain. Using the current rates established by the Committee on Gift Annuities, Mrs. Gregory will receive a guaranteed annual payment of $740 for life, most of which will be tax free. She will receive a substantial charitable gift deduction, and any realized capital gains tax would be spread over her life expectancy.

Setting Up Your Gift Annuity Program

The articles of incorporation or constitution of your organization need to be reviewed and updated. The annuity program should be approved by the board of trustees and supported with an adequate budget. Professional advisors can be used whenever necessary in getting the program properly established. Be certain your program is actuarially sound and approved by your attorney. The well-managed institution will know what it costs to obtain its gifts through annuities and it will be prepared to wait for results.

Administration of the gift annuity program begins before you start receiving gift annuities. You should:

1. Devise a system for processing applications, issuing gift annuity agreements, and supplying proper tax information.

2. Establish a procedure for making payments to annuitants.

3. Plan a follow-up program with gift annuity contract holders.

4. Develop sound policies for managing the investment of gift annuity reserves.

How the gift annuity fund is managed is also very important. Here are three possibilities.

1. *Self-administration*. Your own management handles the investments. Avoid placing the investment responsibilities on one executive. Group judgment of qualified management is essential.

2. *Outside administration*. Hire professional investment managers or have the funds administered by a trust company

under an agency agreement. Check the "track record" of any institution before employing it to handle gift annuity funds.

3. *Reinsure your gift annuities.* Protect your annuitants through a life insurance company by purchasing single premium immediate installment refund annuities. This method will probably be the most expensive but also the safest approach with fewer administrative costs and responsibilities.

To help you decide which investment management plan to use, here is a rule of thumb:

- *If you acquire less than one hundred gift annuities annually, consider guaranteeing them through the purchase of single premium installment refund annuities from carefully selected life insurance companies. There are exceptions to this suggestion, for example, when the institution is well established, has adequate reserves, and is able to handle the administration.*
- *If you receive more than one hundred annuities annually, consider self-administration or a professionally administered plan offered by leading banks.*

Watch Those Rates

Did you hear the story about the frail little lady who some years ago approached a small college to talk about a gift annuity? At her age of 55, the established rate was only about 4 percent. As they talked about her plan to give $100,000 for a gift annuity, she repeatedly pointed out how poor her health had been all of her life. She told them she wanted 9 percent. She appeared weak because she talked with difficulty and had a hacking cough. Her sister had died at age 70 with tuberculosis. At age 55, and weighing only about 90 pounds, she seemed a "good" risk. The management decided to give her the rate of 9 percent a year because they didn't believe she would live very long, and besides, bonds were currently yielding 5½ percent.

In five years they wondered if they had made a mistake.

In ten years they began to worry about their liability.

In twenty years they called a meeting to discuss how they

141

would handle her payments and finally decided to buy a commercial annuity from a life insurance company to cover their liability.

So be careful, don't be too eager to take some annuities offered to you by individuals who want special consideration. These people may live much longer than you expected.

What Will It Cost?

Now let's talk about administration costs. On the surface, using a life insurance company seems to be the most expensive way of guaranteeing annuity payments. But it is also the most certain way and requires the least amount of administration.

If you hire a trust company under an agency arrangement, there will be a continuing fee, but it is possible you will have more of the original sum left at the death of the annuitant.

When you self-administer your program, it is seemingly less expensive; however, the value of management's time must be determined, and management must possess the "know-how" required to invest gift annuity reserves.

In my judgment the self-administered plan is the least desirable because in many charitable institutions, the management team is often so highly oriented to the program or mission of the institution that they rarely have expertise in investments.

Here is a good place to consider costs and values. A poor investment program can cost little in fees and other visible expenses, but it costs everything if an inexperienced management makes unwise investment decisions.

John Ruskin, nineteenth-century English writer and critic, said, "When you pay too much for something, it costs you a little money; but when you pay too little for something that will not do the job for which it was intended, it costs you everything."

A Permit May Be Required

Some states require a permit to offer gift annuities. If in doubt about which states have such laws, check with the Committee on Gift Annuities. Further information on permits is included in Appendix 2 beginning on page 211.

Who Are Prospects?

What about prospects for gift annuities? Who are they? Generally speaking, they are females over 45 from all walks of life.

A good profile would be a single woman (nurse, school teacher, businesswoman, or widow), age 70, without dependents, with a donative intent, and who is a donor or ex-donor to your institution. She probably owns some stocks, including mutual funds that have appreciated in value but are producing inadequate income. She may be afraid to sell her stocks for fear she will lose her security or have to pay an enormous capital gains tax. She will have confidence in the institution and believe its work is essential.

How do you find these prospects? First, go to your board of trustees, to your top 110 donors, and to all the people these groups influence. Go to staff members with long tenure. Get names, ages, and referrals to as many of their friends as possible.

Second, start a direct mail program to your entire donors list and test your former donors to determine whether or not they are potential gift annuitants. Make quarterly mailings to the prospects you locate for as long as two years. Support your direct mail campaign with articles and ads in institutional publications directed to your donors.

How do you deal with prospects when you find them? This depends on how the contacts are made. In personal contacts, you simply furnish the rate of payment and tax benefits for a given age and examine carefully the type of property being exchanged for the gift annuity. Beware of offers of apartment buildings, motels, unimproved property, and other nonmarketable properties. Be reluctant to exchange gift annuities for real estate in cities experiencing a lack of growth because of military or industrial relocation.

In the case of prospects developed through direct mail, they will usually be high-interest people who are able to make gifts through gift annuities, and all you need to do is answer their questions.

143

When answering inquiries, be sure to furnish specific information that will answer any questions raised. When making a reply, include an application form with instructions and a business reply envelope. Sometimes it is desirable to follow up immediately by telephone. Many organizations have a reasonable flow of gift annuities coming in from their direct mail and advertising efforts alone. Recently, a coupon from a brochure was received by one of our client institutions. The potential donor had scribbled on the coupon, "I have $10,000 which I will give to another institution if I don't hear from you soon." The planned giving officer wisely got on the telephone and completed the gift without a visit.

Follow-Up

How do you follow up? Be alert to the incoming mail. When a person tells you that he has a certain stock, is 72 years old, is married, and is interested in providing income for himself and his wife for as long as either of them lives—but he fails to give his wife's age, this is a good natural opening for further contact.

The follow-up I recommend is to telephone him as quickly as possible for the purpose of clarifying his request. Ask for his date of birth and the date of birth of his wife.

Once this information is in hand, write a letter giving specific answers and any other information he may have requested. With this letter, send along a proposal form with all the pertinent information, which was also included in the body of your letter.

Most of your inquiries are not of the quality mentioned above, but are simply coupons showing a date of birth. These responses require longer development. Many times the contact with the person is built by mail over a period of years.

Some people take more than one annuity. I can think of one person who has given twenty-two annuities in the last six years to the same institution. The face amount of these gifts exceeds $100,000. When an attempt was made to visit her, she refused to see anyone, but she continues to send her annuities without personal contact from that institution.

I recall another situation in which a person wrote a letter and asked for the amount of payment on a joint and survivorship annuity and the individual rates for his wife and himself. We simply followed this up by mail.

A year later when we visited this couple in person we learned that another institution had called on them in the meantime and had made arrangements for annuity contracts and other deferred gifts totaling several hundred thousand dollars.

This donor has been faithful in sending $10,000 to the first institution on a regular basis for more annuities, but a golden opportunity to secure the larger gifts was missed because of our failure to make proper follow up.

Another donor I know has so many gift annuities for large amounts that he takes the payments he receives quarterly from the many charitable institutions and uses them to establish new gift annuities every three months!

Maybe you will discover donors like this "sleeping" in your files. They will "raise their hands" if you establish a properly developed charitable gift annuity program for your institution.

Chapter Twelve
The Ways People Give—Now *and* Later
Part 2: Charitable Remainder Annuity Trusts • Charitable Remainder Unitrusts • Charitable Income Trusts • Pooled Income Funds

While a 70-year-old donor may be very happy with a gift annuity returning annual payments at a 6.8 percent rate, a younger counterpart might not be interested at all.

Because gift annuity rates are based on the age of the giver at the time the gift is made, gift annuities definitely have an appeal that grows with age! The older the giver, the higher the annual rate of payment. (A 40-year-old donor, for instance, would receive only 4.8 percent of his gift annuity as an annual payment.)

So what does your institution have to offer the younger donor who also would like to make a gift and provide an income?

Charitable Remainder Annuity Trust

You might suggest the charitable remainder annuity trust, a product of the Tax Reform Act of 1969, which gives the donor a fixed return of at least 5 percent of the fair market value of the trust *when it is established*. The rate *could* be higher—an amount agreed upon by the donor and the trustee. But once established, the percentage rate never changes.

These payments continue to the donor, if he is the named

beneficiary, or to anyone designated, for life or a period of time not to exceed twenty years. At the death of the last income beneficiary or the end of the term of years, the assets in the trust are turned over to your institution as stipulated in the trust agreement.

Here's How It Works

Let's assume Mr. Bartlett, 63, has $100,000 worth of securities he purchased three years ago for $50,000. These securities are only yielding an average of 2 percent. He has an adjusted gross income of $40,000 and is anxious to make a gift and provide himself with a fixed income for life without having to pay any capital gains tax on the appreciation of his securities.

One possible solution might be for Mr. Bartlett to transfer the $100,000 into a charitable remainder annuity trust with the percentage rate to be set at 6 percent. This means Mr. Bartlett would be entitled to receive $6,000 per year for the rest of his life regardless of how the assets in the trust fluctuated. In making this gift Mr. Bartlett avoids the capital gains taxes that he normally would have to pay on the $50,000 appreciation in the securities.

In addition, he is entitled to an income tax deduction based on the charitable remainder interest at the time of his gift. Mr. Bartlett may deduct as a charitable contribution approximately 49 percent of the net fair market value of his gift at age 63. Thus, his total deduction would be approximately $49,000, according to established treasury tables.[1]

Gifts of appreciated securities may be deducted up to 30 percent of adjusted gross income, so Mr. Bartlett will be allowed $12,000 income tax deduction in the year of his gift, and the remainder can be deducted in the five successive tax years.

Not to be overlooked is the fact that Mr. Bartlett has succeeded in accomplishing one of his financial objectives by transferring low yield securities that are now converted to return him $6,000 per year for the rest of his life.

It must be kept in mind that income beneficiaries, when

[1]Treasury Regulation 1.664-1(d)(1).

receiving distributions from the trust, will have to report the income each year on their income tax returns. The following is the tier structure establishing guidelines for how beneficiaries will report income. (See Chapter 17 for further explanation.)

1. Ordinary income
2. Capital gains income
3. "Other" or tax exempt income
4. Tax-free return of principal

Funds Are Held Separately

Unlike the gift annuity, the charitable annuity trust funds are held separate from other funds of the institution. If the assets of a certain annuity trust were depleted, which is unlikely, the payments to the donor beneficiary would cease. If the trust earned *more* than the percentage of the payments to the beneficiary, the excess would go back into the principal of the trust.

Charitable remainder annuity trusts may be created during the lifetime or arranged by the will. To insure all of the federal income, gift, and estate tax deductions that one would normally be entitled to when entering into this type of agreement, very strict requirements must be followed when drafting governing instruments.

Development officers should have the donor contact a qualified attorney to prepare the agreement. By qualified, I mean someone who has had experience in the field of estate planning and taxation. The inclusion of or omission of one sentence in a trust instrument not only may cause the donor to lose all of his tax deductions, but may also result in his or her estate having to pay a federal gift tax, even on the gift to the charitable institution.

Let's review some of the important things to remember when talking with a donor or his attorney about the possibilities of setting up a charitable remainder annuity trust.

1. The trustee must pay each year a fixed amount of income to the designated income beneficiary based on a certain percentage of the assets of the trust determined at the time of the initial funding of the trust. The percentage cannot be less

than 5 percent of the net fair market value of the assets at the time of the transfer.

2. The designated beneficiary or beneficiaries must be living at the time the trust is created and the payments must continue for their entire lifetime(s), or for a term of years not to exceed twenty years.

3. A charitable remainder annuity trust may be funded with cash, securities or other property, except tangible personal property. (A charitable deduction is denied if the annuity trust is funded with tangible personal property.) When accepting real property as a means of funding an annuity trust, be sure the property being transferred is not subject to some indebtedess because this might violate the self-dealing and the unrelated-business income rules. This would mean some severe penalties not only for the trust, but possibly for the donor as well.

4. If the trust in any taxable year earns less than its required pay-out return, the trustee must invade the trust principal to fulfill the pay-out requirements.

5. At the death of the last income beneficiary, the trust's assets must go to a qualified charitable institution.

6. No additional contributions can be made to a charitable remainder annuity trust. If you have a donor who is considering a series of gifts subject to some life income, suggest one of the variations of the charitable remainder unitrust that will be discussed later, or suggest that new annuity trusts may be established for each additional gift.

7. The charitable remainder annuity trust must be invested as a separate trust.

Who Are Prospects?

There are a few things to bear in mind when searching for potential prospects for the charitable remainder annuity trust. An individual who wants a specific amount of income for life, which is not tied to inflation or other economic factors, is a good candidate for a charitable remainder annuity trust. Individuals who have large amounts of bonds are also good candidates, because bonds will generally provide the fixed amount the donor wants for his lifetime without jeopardizing the trust or the donor.

Charitable Remainder Unitrust

But let's say that your donor, who wants to make a gift to your institution with income benefits to himself, would like for his payments to follow the economic changes year-by-year. He would like to enjoy a larger return if the trust grows and is willing to accept less if it diminishes in certain years.

A *charitable remainder unitrust* would suit his needs better than either a gift annuity or a charitable remainder annuity trust.

There are three different types of unitrusts, each offering attractive benefits for the donor.

The "Straight" Unitrust

The first type, what we will call the "straight" unitrust, is by definition a separate trust from which a fixed percentage of the net fair market value of the trust assets, *as determined annually*, must be paid to a designated beneficiary or beneficiaries for life, or for a period of time not to exceed twenty years. The stated percentage in the trust must be at least 5 percent.

For example, assume Mr. Woods has $100,000 worth of securities and is interested in some type of investment that will protect him during times of increased inflation. He is also very charitably motivated.

One solution would be to transfer those securities to a "straight" unitrust that would provide that the trustee pay Mr. Woods 6 percent of the net fair market value of the trust assets valued annually. The first year Mr. Woods would be entitled to an income payment of $6,000, that is, 6 percent of the $100,000.

Assume the trust assets in the second year appreciate to $110,000. Mr. Woods would then be entitled to receive $6,600. In the same way, if in the third year the assets of the trust dropped to $90,000, Mr. Woods's payments would only be $5,400.

A "straight" unitrust properly invested can provide both the beneficiaries and the charity with increased benefits. For example, a 6 percent unitrust originally funded with $200,000, realizing a total growth each year of 8 percent, would appreciate in value to around $300,000 in a twenty-year period of time. As the assets of the trust grow, the income the beneficiaries are entitled to each year grows. And the resulting gift to charity is $100,000 more than the original gift. A "straight" unitrust properly invested can be a good vehicle for both the beneficiaries and the charity. (Keep in mind—the trust assets may not grow at all. The value may even decrease.)

The "Net Income" Unitrust

The second variation of the charitable remainder unitrust we will refer to as the "net income" unitrust. This unitrust provides that the trustee pays the donor or other designated beneficiaries an amount equal to a fixed percentage of the net fair market value of the trust assets (not to be less than 5 percent) determined annually or the actual income earned, whichever is less.

For example, assume Mr. Gardner funded a net income unitrust with $100,000 that had a stipulated pay-out rate of 6 percent or the income, whichever was less. If in the first year the trust actually earned only $4,000, then the distribution requirement would be made by paying the $4,000 to Mr. Gardner. If in the second year the trust earned $7,000, then the trustee would pay $6,000 to Mr. Gardner, and the additional $1,000 would become a part of trust principal. The income tax charitable deduction would be determined by using the actuarial tables based on a 6 percent return, or any other percentage stipulated in the trust.

The "Net Income Plus Make-up" Unitrust

The third variation of the charitable remainder unitrust is the "net income plus make-up" unitrust. Under this type of trust arrangement the trustee is directed to pay a fixed percentage of the net fair market value of the trust assets determined annually (not to be less than 5 percent or the income, whichever is less) with an additional provision that in years in which the income earned is greater than the percentage of the fair market value of the assets, those excess earnings can be paid to the extent that they don't exceed the accumulated deficiencies for prior years, that is, years in which the trust earned less than the stated percentage.

Assume Mr. Davis funds a 6 percent income plus make-up unitrust with $100,000 worth of securities. The first year the trust earns $2,000. The second year the trust earns $3,000. In the third year the trust earns $4,000. Based on a $6,000 pay out each year, the trust has accumulated deficiencies of $9,000. In each year the trust pays what is actually earned to Mr. Davis. In the fourth year the trust still valued at $100,000 earns $8,000. The trustee would pay the $6,000 normally due to Mr. Davis plus an additional $2,000 to make up some of the prior deficiencies for the first, second, and third years. Thus in the fourth year the trustee is reducing the deficiencies to $7,000. In future years, when the trust income exceeds the stated percentage, these deficiencies may be further reduced.

There are certain tax advantages to creating a charitable unitrust just as there are for a charitable remainder annuity trust. Unitrusts funded with cash are deductible to the extent that they do not exceed 50 percent of the donor's adjusted gross income. Unitrusts funded with appreciated securities or property are deductible to the extent that they don't exceed 30 percent of the donor's adjusted gross income. When unitrusts are funded with appreciated property the donor avoids all of the capital gains tax.

Let's consider Mr. Swenson, age 68, a widower who funds a 6 percent charitable remainder unitrust with $100,000 worth of securities that cost him $25,000. In order to determine Mr. Swenson's income tax deductions, we must go to the treasury tables to find what percentage of his gift is considered the charitable remainder interest. According to the tables, Mr. Swenson will be entitled to a deduction of approximately 54 percent of the fair market value of the gift, or $54,000. Assuming his adjusted gross income is $50,000 in the year of the gift and for several following years, he will be entitled to a deduction of $15,000 the year of the gift, an additional $15,000 for the next two years following the gift, and then $9,000 in the fourth year after the gift, at which time he will have utilized the full charitable deduction. In the meantime, he will have avoided the capital gains tax that would have been due had the property been disposed of through a normal sale. The income that Mr. Swenson receives under our example will be taxed according to the same tier structure that we discussed for the charitable remainder annuity trust. That is (1) ordinary income, (2) capital gains income, (3) "other" or tax-exempt income, and (4) tax-free return of principal.

Unitrusts Are Very Flexible

Practically every potential substantial donor could make use of a unitrust because of the flexibility of this investment. If a person is looking for a way to receive an income tax deduction during his lifetime and at the same time provide an income for himself or other designated beneficiaries to offset rising infla-tion, the "straight" unitrust might well be the best option. We have seen that as the trust assets increase, so will the benefici-ary's income.

If on the other hand the donor has a need for a current income tax deduction—but no additional income—he may consider funding a net income unitrust. This type of agreement is particularly advantageous when the donor is funding the trust with real property. If for some reason the property cannot be sold for a period of time, the trustee is relieved from any income payments and the donor knows that once the property is sold the assets can be invested in income producing securities.

An often overlooked method of using the net income plus make-up unitrust is in situations where a donor is in a very high income bracket. He has no need for current income but will need additional income after retirement when his income drops substantially.

By properly investing the net income plus make-up unitrust, the trustee may accumulate large amounts of deficiencies that by investment in low-yield growth stocks can be made up later at the donor's retirement by reinvesting the trust assets in high-yield stocks or bonds. When funding a unitrust subject to two lives, one must be careful to include a provision in the trust

153

agreement that will prevent the donor from having to pay an unnecessary federal gift tax. The example we discussed for the annuity trust will suffice. (See page 152.)

As far as federal estate tax laws are concerned, the same rules apply as for a charitable remainder annuity trust. That is, when the donor has funded a one-life agreement and is the beneficiary, the assets will be included in his estate, but will be totally deductible as a charitable contribution. When the donor has funded a two-life agreement the income interest for the surviving beneficiary must be included as part of the taxable estate. A charitable remainder unitrust may also be made during lifetime or as a testamentary gift. Once again, very strict requirements must be followed when drafting these types of instruments.

Let's review some of the most important things to remember with respect to charitable remainder unitrusts:

1. A unitrust may be funded with cash, securities, or real property. Do not fund a unitrust with tangible personal property as the charitable deduction will be disallowed. Also, be careful about accepting property that is subject to some type of indebtedness, as once again, the trust and the donor might be subject to self-dealing and unrelated-business income penalties.

2. The income payments must be made at least annually based on fixed percentage not to be less than 5 percent of the net fair market value of the assets, as determined annually.

3. The income beneficiary or beneficiaries designated in the trust must be living at the time the gift is made. The trust must run for the lives of the beneficiary or beneficiaries, or for a specific term of years not to exceed twenty.

4. Unlike the charitable remainder annuity trust, additional contributions may be made to the charitable remainder unitrust. However, in order to assure the deduction the donor is entitled to, there must be a provision in the governing instrument outlining the procedure for valuing these additional gifts.

5. The unitrust is a separate agreement and must be invested as such.

6. At the termination of the trust, the assets must go to a qualified charitable institution as defined in Section 170 of the Internal Revenue Code.

Charitable Income Trusts

The charitable income trust is known by three other names: a charitable lend trust, a short term charitable trust, and a reversionary trust.

This trust is created for a term of years (more than ten years) by a trustor who transfers certain income producing assets to a trustee with instructions to pay the income earned to a charitable institution during the term of the trust.

Under the 1969 Tax Reform Act, the donor is not allowed a charitable deduction for any gift of income unless he is treated as the owner of the income interest. In other words, the income is taxed to him. In order to receive the charitable income tax deduction, the income interest must take the form of either a unitrust or an annuity trust. The income must be stated as a percent of the initial net fair market value of the funds placed in the trust when an annuity trust is used. In the case of a unitrust, the income must be a fixed percentage of the fair market value of the trust assets determined annually.

Pooled Income Fund

But what if your donor wants a flexible income from his gift (ruling out a gift annuity), but doesn't want to tie up as much as a separate trust might require?

A pooled income fund might be the answer—another way he may give now *and* later.

The pooled income fund is a trust to which a donor transfers property irrevocably to or for the use of a qualified charitable institution and retains an income. Each donor's gift property is commingled with property transferred by other donors who have made similar gifts. The income is determined by the rate of return earned by the trust each year and is paid for the life of one or two persons living at the time of such transfer, prorated according to each donor's share of the fund.

The trust is maintained by the institution to which the

remainder interest is contributed but may have a bank or some other financial corporation as trustee. At the death of the donor, the principal of the trust attributable to that donor is used by the charitable institution.

Pooled income giving will be most attractive to donors with smaller amounts of money that would normally be insufficient to fund a charitable trust—where the funds have to be invested separately.

Gifts of $1,000, $5,000, $10,000 or perhaps even $25,000 could be considered for the pooled income fund. In most situations, a trustee would be reluctant to take a unitrust or annuity trust of this size because of the problems of investing as a separate trust. The administrative requirements and reporting requirements involved would also be cumbersome.

The 1969 Tax Reform Act altered the mechanics and requirements of a pooled income fund trust. *It serves as a great vehicle for attracting small donors that would ordinarily be reluctant to contribute assets irrevocably without some kind of income return.* It must be remembered that the pooled income fund is an irrevocable instrument and anything transferred can never be taken back by the donor.

Going to Market

From the marketing standpoint, you might look to some of your thousand dollar and above contributors, as well as those who have taken out charitable gift annuities in the past. One feature of the pooled income fund that will be more attractive than the charitable gift annuity is the fact that the capital gains tax on appreciated property can be avoided completely, whereas some will be incurred under the charitable gift annuity agreement.

However, under the pooled income fund rules, all of the income received by the income beneficiary will be taxable as ordinary income. The very idea that an individual will have an income for life, no matter how small, is often the key to securing a pooled income fund gift. Many people also like the idea of having their money invested in some type of pool as opposed to asking a trustee to maintain individual investment policies where one bad stock could cause a great loss in the trust.

The investment goal of the pooled income fund may be more "growth" oriented than the investment policy of the charitable remainder unitrust.

The pooled income fund benefits the donor and the institution in several ways:

1. Donor gives to your institution now.

2. Donor receives variable life income that will be reported as ordinary income.

3. Donor avoids capital gains tax.

4. Donor is allowed an income tax deduction the year the gift is made.

5. Donor saves administration and other estate settlement costs at death (since this is a contract it is not includable in donor's estate for probate purposes).

6. Institution's management is aided in long-range planning.

7. Institution gets "foot in the door" for a future estate planning opportunity.

How to Develop These Now-*and*-Later Gifts

The most important thing about getting donors to contribute to your institution through a charitable remainder annuity trust, a charitable remainder unitrust, or the pooled income fund is to let them know you have such plans.

You can make this known by the use of brochures, booklets, articles, advertisements, and whatever other vehicles you have for communicating with your donors.

The brochures, booklets, or other publications should not contain any extreme promises, such as guaranteeing a tax-free income for life or a great investment return. Most of these simply will not happen.

As in other types of planned gifts, you are looking for a better way for people to give who are already motivated to support your institution.

Initial articles about giving-for-income plans may be very general and may not even mention the names of the various plans, but they can simply tell what can be accomplished for the donor as well as for the institution.

Details can wait for the interested prospective giver. It is probably sufficient to tell your donors they *can* make a gift now, receive an income for life, claim tax advantages, and benefit your institution with a final gift at death. Tell them this—and I will almost guarantee some will say, "That's for me!"

Chapter Thirteen
The Ways People Give—Now *and* Later Part 3: Revocable Living Trusts

A revocable living trust is an agreement entered into by a person or persons and a trustee desiring to accomplish the following:

• To provide for the payment of income to the donor *or* to your institution.

• To assure the donor he may have the assets of the agreement returned upon request.

• To transfer the assets to the beneficiaries at death without going through probate court. *The beneficiary could, of course, be your institution.*

Simply stated, a revocable gift is one the donor can take back. Why does an institution want this kind of gift? There are several good reasons.

We sometimes think the alternative to a revocable planned gift is an irrevocable planned gift. This is not always true. Often a donor's alternative to making a revocable planned gift is *no gift at all*.

I have heard leaders of charitable institutions say: "I wouldn't want revocable agreements, because you never know if you've got a gift."

That's true.

An officer of an institution told me with some satisfaction, "We have more than $10 million in deferred gifts and we don't have a single revocable living trust."

I thought, "You would probably have $30 million if you *did* have revocable gifts." It is necessary to include in planned giving programs "vehicles" of giving that make it possible for donors to give *now*, reserving the right to have their gifts returned in whole or in part.

My experience has been that most people don't revoke revocable living trusts. One institution I know has received more than $20 million in revocable living trusts and only a few (less than five percent) have been revoked. However, with the uncertainties in life that we all face, many people are not really sure whether they can afford to give the amount of money they would like to give to your institution. This is where the revocable living trust is a vital "tool" of charitable estate planning.

Many institutions throughout the United States have found that revocable living trusts are great plans for generating larger-than-average charitable gifts, but other institutions are still overlooking this gift source.

Some institutions are reluctant to encourage revocable living trust gifts because they fear the donor will revoke the agreement. The donor may get angry and withdraw the assets and give them to another institution he suddenly likes better. This is a possibility and happens when the donor believes the institution has changed its goals and methods. And since the institution has gone to some expense in establishing the agreement, it is left "holding the bag."

But in my experience, revocable living trusts are rarely revoked when properly understood. Two reasons donors revoke these agreements are (1) they are dissatisfied with changes in your institution's mission, or (2) they have a change in their economic situation requiring the use of some or all of the funds in the trust.

If a person needs part or all of what he has given on this basis, I prefer to be able to return it immediately. I do not believe we have the right to grasp gifts of this type when in so doing we take away the person's economic freedom and financial security.

It would disturb me to think of some institutional representative coming to see my mother, for instance, and tying up all of her assets in an irrevocable agreement. I want her to have options. I want her to be free. Isn't that what we want for every donor?

Please don't think I am opposed to *irrevocable* planned gifts. They are fine when they help the person give, obtain tax benefits, and do not impair the person's economic freedom or planned security.

Advantages to the Institution

Larger Gifts

The institution normally receives a larger-than-average-size planned gift when it is in the form of a revocable gift. The gift is readily available to the donor during life and for the use of the institution at death. Oftentimes part or all of the assets in revocable living trusts are withdrawn and given to the institution outright or for a gift annuity or some other plan offering tax advantages. A revocable gift is sometimes the lead-in to receiving an entire estate. The average size gift coming in through a revocable living trust may be ten times larger than your average bequest through a will.

Readily Available Gifts

A revocable living trust makes the donor's gift readily available at death. (Since revocable gift arrangments are contracts, the assets pass to the charity outside the donor's will. In fact, a contract-type gift takes precedence over the will. These agreements help cut down on probate expenses and unnecessary delays.)

Possibility of Other Types of Gifts

As mentioned above, donors sometimes transfer their trust assets to the institution as current gifts or exchange these assets for gift annuities, annuity trusts, unitrusts, life income contracts, charitable income trusts, or turn them into irrevocable life estate contracts.

Donor Commitment

Valuable personal contact is established and can be maintained with significant donors who are highly motivated to give and can be encouraged to respond to needs of the institution from time to time. I believe the revocable gift donor is possibly more committed than the irrevocable gift donor because the former is more than likely placing a greater part of his own personal assets on the line in the event of death.

Increased Current Gifts

An institution may be able to inspire an increase in the donor's current giving by showing how to establish a regular giving plan through assignment of part or all of the income from the revocable living trust for a definite project or time. Or, the donor may give the principal outright.

One donor gave property worth more than $50,000 to an institution in a revocable living trust. Within two years, he decided to give the trust assets outright to that institution for use in its current budget.

Tax Considerations

Since these gifts are revocable, there are no current tax advantages. But keep in mind that tax deductions are not the prime motivator in charitable giving. I believe it is very rare indeed when a donor gives solely for the tax deductions.

Who Can Be the Trustee?

The trustee can be a bank, in some cases a charitable institution, or an individual. This will depend on state laws and the wishes of the one establishing the trust.

Who Needs a Revocable Living Trust?

Persons owning property of various kinds, securities, leases, notes, mortgages, land contracts, or any other personal property, who have a desire to give this property to a charitable institution at death, might want to give now, but they cannot dispose of the property while they live because they may need the income. It is also possible the donor will need to use some or all of the principal before death. By entering into a revocable living trust, a person can retain the income for himself and retain the right to withdraw any portion. Whatever remains at death will pass to the charitable beneficiary.

Beneficiaries

There are two kinds of trust beneficiaries: the beneficiary of income and the beneficiary of the principal. The donor may name himself, a dependent, or your institution to receive the income and may name another person or your institution to receive the principal at death.

The payment of the income to the donor (or the designated beneficiary) may be made annually, semiannually, quarterly, or within a period of time from date of receipt. The income may be accumulated or paid as agreed by the parties.

The revocable living trust agreement is a "vehicle" for transferring property to an institution with the least expense and minimum delay. The property does not pass through the donor's will. Since the donor receives the income and has the right to revoke, maximum security is retained. In addition to this, group management, which may be much better for him than self-management, is secured. (Elderly people, especially, often want the help of a competent financial advisor.) One other very important value to many donors is the privacy of the gift—a revocable living trust is not public information.

Investment of Funds

Although the revocable living trust agreement provides that donors will receive the assets in the agreement at the time of revocation, the usual intent of the donor is to invest the funds in such a way that little fluctuation will be experienced. There are exceptions, however. Some will want you to invest it for maximum income; others will suggest a more aggressive position, or just that you hold the investments they've already made.

The institution can accept revocable gifts under two plans. In the first, the donor retains the investment control. This may be desirable in some cases, especially when he owns stocks he really likes. For example, a donor may have stocks that are highly appreciated and wants to keep them. You, as trustee, may not want to retain them for one reason or another. Because he gets the desired income by taking the small dividends and withdrawing a few shares as needed, he is content to keep them.

The second—more ideal—way of accepting revocable gifts is to have the institution's investment committee in charge of the investment and reinvestment of all funds. It is possible to establish a pool for the investment of such funds.

Even though redemptions may be exceeding new investments in mutual funds, we should not overlook the tremendous impact the funds are making on our society and could make on our institutions. More and more people are wanting to own stocks and often they select mutual funds. These funds are suited for revocable living trusts and can even be set up by the mutual fund organization with the individual serving as his own trustee.

An Example

Here's how one couple used a revocable living trust and life insurance to *triple* their gift! Mr. and Mrs. Morehouse, ages 43 and 42, transferred to a charitable revocable trust $20,000 of corporate bonds with coupons paying $1,600 a year. They wanted the bonds held in trust until they needed them. They were giving the income to the charity until further notice. Mr. and Mrs. Morehouse wanted the $20,000 principal to go to the charity at the death of the last survivor.

With this information in mind, the trustee was authorized to purchase a $20,000 joint ordinary life insurance policy on their lives. The policy provided, at the death of the first, that $20,000 would be paid to the charity. The life insurance policy included a provision making it possible for the survivor to continue the same amount of insurance without presenting any new evidence of insurability. At the death of the survivor, a second $20,000 would go to the charity. In addition to these two $20,000 life insurance gifts, the assets remaining in the trust would go to the charity.

Summary of the Plan

1. Trust is created with $20,000 of corporate bonds.

2. Income of $1,600 is a gift to the charity. A sum of $680 is used to purchase a $20,000 joint ordinary life insurance policy with the charitable institution as irrevocable owner and beneficiary. The premiums are deductible and the cash values belong to the charity.

3. At the death of the first person, $20,000 goes to charity from the life insurance.

4. At the death of the second person, $20,000 goes to charity from insurance, plus the trust assets of $20,000.

5. Donors have been allowed a $1,600 annual income tax deduction as a contribution and they have reserved the right to revoke the trust and have all the principal returned.

Prospects

The best prospects for revocable gifts are

1. People who are not sure of their financial futures.

2. Last members of families. We sometimes find single women who are aged and are without beneficiaries.

3. Retired couples without children.

4. Teachers, nurses, widows, widowers—young and old —may start a charitable giving program of significance.

Revocable living trusts are completed in face-to-face interviews rather than by a telephone call or through correspondence. There are many people who want to give in this way. In fact, *there are people who will only give in this way*. I therefore urge you to gear your program for the purpose of securing substantial gifts through the various revocable giving plans.

Chapter Fourteen
Special Giving Resources

With real estate values soaring, the ownership of a home or farm becomes more significant in terms of financial resources. Many of your donors, perhaps, are wondering what will become of their homes or farms when they die. Others, who have a high motivation to give more to your institution, believe they cannot give because all of their assets are tied up in real property.

Regular reminders that your institution can receive and make good use of such property is often enough to stimulate such gifts, especially when the giver knows that he can give his home now (if the gift is irrevocable, certain immediate tax benefits are obtainable), and yet continue to live there the rest of his life.

Three Types of Real Estate Gifts

Home or Farm: the Life Estate Contract

The life estate contract is an agreement between a donor and the institution providing for the transfer of a donor's home or family farm to the institution with the giver reserving for himself a life estate. The life estate gives the donor the right to live in or on the property, receive the income, pay taxes and insurance, and maintain the property during life.

It is simply a written agreement between a donor and the institution. The property is deeded to the institution and registered in the county registrar of deed's office. The deed includes a life estate provision. The life estate contract merely recognizes the deed and stipulates the terms of the agreement.

The responsibility of the institution is limited. The donor has the owner's rights while he lives. (Note: this type of arrangement should be carefully worked out by the donor's attorney. The institution should also determine if it has any liability.)

The prospects are limited to those persons owning homes or family farms who want to give the property to the institution when they die. Couples without children and single men and women (especially last members of the family) are excellent prospects.

The benefits to the donor include:

1. Donor makes a gift now that takes effect at death.
2. Probate expense is avoided.
3. Donor lives on the property for life.
4. Donor has the satisfaction of knowing the property will benefit the charitable institution when he dies.
5. When the title is passed irrevocably to the institution on this basis, the donor is allowed an income tax deduction for a gift even though he uses the property or income therefrom for as long as he lives. However, the donor should be quite certain that he will not need to use any of the principal during his lifetime.

The benefits to the institution include:

1. The property passes to your institution without going through the probate courts. (This statement is general; the laws of each state must be applied.)
2. Title to the property usually comes much quicker through this arrangement than through a will.
3. The cost of securing title to the property through the life estate contract should be much less than receiving a gift through the will since many of the estate settlement costs will not apply.
4. When the life estate contract is revocable, it is often a first step toward making a substantial current gift or an irrevocable gift. Revocable arrangements help donors retain their economic freedom.

Generally speaking, a life estate contract produces a much larger gift than a bequest. Some donors, when making a final gift to a charitable institution they have supported over the years, prefer to give real property because they tend to consider their real estate "sacred."

EXAMPLE: Mr. and Mrs. Arnold owned a home on a small family farm. They had been able to derive a good living and had made substantial charitable gifts over the years. They decided to continue farming temporarily and to later transfer title to the farm to the charitable institution, reserving a life estate on a revocable basis. About two years later, they decided to quit farming, retire, and move to another state. They asked the institution I represented to accept the farm as an outright gift, to sell it, and to place the proceeds in some special projects in which they were interested.

Once we had clear title, we placed the farm on the market and sold it, receiving more than $40,000. This money was placed in the project they had designated, and the Arnolds expressed their deep satisfaction in the plans they had completed.

Giving Rental or Other Business Real Estate for a Lifetime Income

It is also possible for a donor to give rental or other business real estate to your institution in exchange for an income for life. The amount of income is based both on the age of the giver at the time of the transaction and the fair market value of the property.

The income may be fixed or variable, depending on the needs of the donor.

Giving Rental or Other Business Real Estate Outright

Sometimes donors who are advanced in age decide they do not want the responsibility of maintaining a home or caring for rental property. They may not need the income and will transfer the title to your institution as an outright gift.

How to Encourage Such Gifts

Inform your public that gifts of real estate are accepted on any of the above bases. Sample contracts appear in Appendixes 7 and 8. These forms are samples only and should never be used without the advice of your attorney. Laws may vary by state.

Other Types of Gifts

There is almost no limit to what *can* be given to your institution.

Here are some additional suggestions that can be conveyed to your clientele along with an emphasis on the more common gift plans, such as we already have discussed—wills, gift annuities, trusts, life insurance, and securities.

Business Inventories

Sometimes corporations acquire surplus inventory that will have to be written off as a loss, but which might very well be used by your institution. Such things as food items, clothing, household supplies, cleaning equipment, camping equipment, and office supplies can be given to your institution; and the corporation can deduct the cost basis (what it cost to produce the inventory plus other costs attributable to owning the product) as a charitable gift. (If items are used in the care of the ill, the needy, or children, the corporation can deduct half of the increased value in addition to the cost basis.)

Cattle, Other Livestock, or Crops

The farmer or rancher may have most of his resources invested in livestock or crops, but these, too, can be given by the motivated donor. Due to market factors, storage problems, feeding expenses, or tax benefits, a farmer who wants to make a special gift to your institution may wish to consider giving livestock or agricultural products. (A tax advisor should be consulted about the specific gift being considered.)

Assigning Royalties for Minerals, Inventions, or Writings

Investors in oil, inventors, writers, or musicians may want to consider giving part or all of their royalties on a certain item or work during a certain year. Or they might choose to pledge royalties for three, five, or ten years. (A tax advisor should be consulted for such gifts.)

Antiques, Paintings, Stamp or Coin Collections

The collector who wants his efforts and investments to be used now for charitable interests, may make a gift of his collection to your institution. The institution may be able to use certain items, such as collections of books or works of art, or it may choose to sell the collection and benefit by the proceeds. (A tax advisor should be consulted about the possible gift deductions allowed.)

Memorial Giving—Daily Income That Meets Three Needs

A successful memorial giving program can be one of the most productive public relations endeavors your institution incorporates in its financial development and donor development efforts.[1]

We consider it here along with planned giving, because it is a multi-purpose type of gift made by people who benefit along with the institution. A memorial gift is one made by a friend of your institution to honor the memory of a deceased person. While many such gifts are made immediately on notice of death, other memorial gifts are continued on a regular basis in the same name for months and even years.

Memorial giving accomplishes three major benefits:

1. It gives the donor a practical avenue for expressing his personal feeling in the loss of a friend or loved one. It helps him fulfill a responsibility.

2. It brings a measure of comfort to the bereaved family, as they receive word of the gift made in memory of the deceased.

3. It provides support for your institution, support which is essentially unsolicited, and which probably will be repeated at the time of other deaths in the future.

A key to the success of a memorial giving program is an alert

---

[1]The material on memorial gifts is taken from the manual "How to Increase Your Income Through Memorial Gifts" by Franklin Robbie. Published by Robert F. Sharpe & Co., Inc. See page 285 for information on obtaining this publication.

staff who will produce immediate action on each memorial gift as it is received. Here are some important factors:

- The bereaved family must receive notice of the gift (not the amount) as soon as possible; some make it a policy to get the gift notice in the next mail.
- The giver must receive a receipt and thank you note explaining that the sympathy card notifying the bereaved family of his gift has been sent by your institution.
- Appropriate recognition should be given in your house publication showing the names of those memorialized and the names of the givers, but again, no reference to the size of the gift.
- Regular and frequent reminders of your memorial gift program should be included in your house publication, as enclosures with other mail, in ads (both space and one-liners), and anywhere else where appropriate. A memorial gift coupon or form makes it easy for your donors to make their gifts. These forms should be sent to them, certainly with their receipts and at frequent intervals.

A memorial giving program offers three specific advantages to your institution:

1. A memorial gift brings immediate cash. You can use it now.

2. Since these gifts cannot be personally solicited, you do not need field staff to develop them. They are volunteered by people who want to give.

3. The names received (those to whom sympathy cards are sent) become high quality additions to your mailing list; they will have a special interest in the work of your institution. Identification with the good work your institution is doing can become a lifelong satisfaction to them.

Yes, We Know . . .

There are obviously some financial development techniques and giving plans that we purposefully have not included in this book. This is in part because these are such highly specialized methods and partly because there is a wealth of other material available on the "how to's" of capital campaigns, annual drives, neighborhood canvassing, telethons, walkathons, direct mail appeals (including the offer of premium gifts), mementos, greeting cards, and so on. All of these have their success stories, or charities would not continue using them.

But we believe the institution that will devote itself to the careful development of *planned* givers, along with a balanced program of public relations and direct mail, will not need to rely on crisis appeals or gimmicks to generate support.

Chapter Fifteen
Charitable Estate Planning

It is often unwise for a person to make a substantial outright gift to a charitable institution without first knowing how the making of the gift affects his overall financial situation.

A few years ago I worked with a businessman who was a board member of a small church-related college. He decided to make an outright gift of $30,000 to the college. But before completing the gift, he took a hard look at his business and personal responsibilities and found by making the gift he could possibly be placing a financial hardship on himself and adversely affecting his income-producing ability. On advice of his CPA, he instead made a pledge of $300 a month for ten years.

A careful analysis of one's estate can affect a person while he lives and have important ramifications after his death. A completed estate plan often helps a donor understand how he can give more than he ever expected he could.

Through charitable estate planning it is possible to help a person arrange his estate so that he protects himself and his family. The charitable estate planning approach is the ultimate in professional fund raising because you literally go out *to help a person give* intelligently and significantly rather than going out to get a gift.

If I were directing a financial development program in an institution, I would be reluctant to employ any planned giving representative to make field calls unless I believed he could be taught how to use the estate analysis approach with the institution's donors.

The time is rapidly passing when an institution can legitimately spend salaries and expenses on a person who crisscrosses the country talking to people about giving through wills, gift annuities, trusts, and other vehicles of giving without being able to help the person, work with his own professional advisors, and make application to the prospect's overall estate needs.

Two Types of Representatives—Take Your Pick

Let's look at two planned giving representatives who are now at work for well-known charitable institutions.

Planned giving officer A is age 50 and has been in planned giving for seven years. He is in a second career. He is personable, works hard, and has his office in his home. His training has consisted of a single two-day planned giving seminar. He attends an annual meeting sponsored by his institution and a national fund raising conference each year.

He has a list of the donors in his territory and receives leads from the home office periodically. He drives everywhere—approximately fifty thousand miles annually. He does not make appointments. He gets in his car, arrives in an area, and knocks on the doors of his donors. Mr. A is liked by the donors and he has many "fellowship" visits. He sees himself as a goodwill ambassador and trouble-shooter for the institution. He is not results-oriented and he tends to study taxation rather than marketing.

Including his salary and expenses, he is costing the institution about $35,000 a year. I suspect he sits behind the wheel of his automobile a full two days a week and averages less than $200,000 of planned gifts each year. At best, planned giving officer A is a marginal representative.

Planned giving officer B is age 33 and has been a planned giving representative for three years. He has attended eleven two- or three-day seminars. He attended a two-week course in estate planning at a well-known university. He reads everything he can find on marketing and charitable estate planning and has an ongoing study program on estates and trusts on which he spends thirty minutes daily.

Mr. B uses the mails, articles, ads, estate planning workshops, and wills clinics (see page 117) to find leads. Through letters and telephone calls he qualifies his leads. He works only by appointment. He makes fewer calls than Mr. A, but in almost every interview he attempts to lead the prospect into estate analysis. He meets the donor's attorney, CPA, life insurance agent, or broker. He makes suggestions in writing.

Mr. B rarely uses his automobile in traveling. He spends his travel money on airplane tickets, hotels, rental cars, and taxis. He is a professional. He knows when his own knowledge is insufficient and uses competent counsel frequently.

While his first efforts in the field yielded very little, during the first three years he developed more than $5 million of gift annuities, trusts, and current gifts. He knows of many wills that have been written in favor of his institution, but he chooses not to include bequests in his production figures until the gift is received at the death of the donor. During his first three years, only two donors he had solicited died leaving money to his institution.

When an institution decides to establish a new program or reorganize an existing program, I am convinced the program should be designed and built around planned giving officers of Mr. B's type. One effective B type is better than ten A-type persons.

In this chapter I am attempting to show how to have an effective program staffed by B-type persons.

Definitions

What is estate planning? It is the process of setting up a plan for the creation, accumulation, conservation, and distribution of one's possessions so that these possessions will do the most for a person and his family if the income producer becomes permanently disabled, dies before providing adequately for his family, retires, or has a temporary emergency seriously affecting his financial well-being.

175

What is an estate plan? It is a blueprint of a financial plan or a bridge that takes a person and his heirs safely over all sorts of dangerous and costly pitfalls . . . such as a long-term disability that may lead to forced retirement.

The institution desiring to use the estate analysis approach needs to consider the following:

1. The board of trustees must decide to launch such a program. The first step is to make certain it is planned well. Employ competent legal counsel and qualified staff, and appropriate an adequate budget to fund the program for at least three years. Forward-looking boards will have the patience to wait for results.

2. Provide office space for the planned giving staff.

3. Spend money on training for all personnel.

4. Establish an effective public relations program designed to create a climate for giving and for producing leads.

5. Have a plan for qualifying leads.

6. Work by appointment.

7. Conduct interviews with prospects and their professional advisors.

8. Establish a follow-up plan.

A Classic Case

It is appropriate here to cite a classic example of how the estate planning approach is used.

This story is told by a woman who was interested in an institution I represented. I believe she has learned what many people never experience: how to enjoy money. This is what she shared with me about herself:

"Finally, I quit procrastinating about making my will. I am 63 years old and never had a will until last year. My father, my mother, and my husband all died without wills.

"So, in light of all I had experienced, read, and heard, I decided to make my will. My lawyer wrote it simply. I left my property to two aunts, a close friend, and some institutions I had supported for years. The lawyer mentioned to me the possibility of needing a trust. Later I decided that this was a good suggestion.

"Then I saw an article in an institution's magazine offering information about a 'unitrust.' I decided to find out more about it. The director of planned giving of that institution came to see me and helped me understand the functions of a unitrust. My lawyer and I visited with him. The plan we developed together gave me confidence that my wishes were being cared for now and in the future in the wisest possible way.

"The planned giving director's first question was, 'Who are the people you would like to care for?'

"My answer was *myself*. I am age 63, my aunt Beth is age 87, another aunt, Mary, is age 85, and Constance, a friend, is 65.

"Next, we listed the property I own:

	Current Value	Cost	Annual Income
Home (no mortgage)	$40,000	$30,000	None
Cash in savings at 5½%	30,000	30,000	$1,650
Land 160 acres	80,000	15,000	1,000 net
Growth mutual fund at 3%	44,000	56,000	1,320
Office equipment stock at 4%	32,000	30,000	1,280
Life Insurance	3,000	Premiums	None
	$229,000	$161,000	$5,250
Social Security Income			$3,400
Total income			$8,650

"Then, we listed the plans I have for my property:

1. Provide for myself for as long as I live.
2. Increase my income.
3. Management of my assets if I am disabled.
4. Provide $200 a month income to each of my two aunts for their lifetimes beginning at my death.
5. Give Constance $100 a month for life beginning at my death.
6. Under my will, 25 percent of the residue goes to a Christian institution that I have supported, 20 percent to my local church, 30 percent to a foreign mission, and 25 percent to a college.

"Finally, we decided how my goals could be accomplished. After discussions with the planned giving director, my lawyer and my financial advisor made recommendations about my property to me in writing. I accepted most of the suggestions and here is what I decided to do:

1. Invest $20,000 of my cash in U.S. Government bonds yielding about 8¼ percent per year. Income $1,650 a year.
2. Sell the $44,000 of mutual funds yielding 3 percent and invest the proceeds in corporate bonds yielding 8½ percent. Income $3,740 a year.
3. Retain the $32,000 of office equipment stock yielding 4 percent. Income $1,280 a year.
4. Place the land in a charitable remainder unitrust that pays me all the income earned up to 6½ percent. Should income be less than this amount for a few years, I would get extra income to make up the deficit in those years when and if, in the future, the trust investments earn more than the 6½ percent of the value of the trust. One of the benefits of this kind of trust is the way the income is paid. It varies each year based on the value of the trust assets. It should help with future inflation. Income up to $5,200 a year.

"Oh, yes, I didn't have to pay a large capital gains tax when I made the gift to the trust. (The land, now valued at $80,000, only cost me $15,000 when I bought it, but had I sold it myself the increase would have been subject to capital gains tax.) Besides, I was allowed nearly $30,000 as an income tax deduction for the gift. This was more than I could deduct the first year. I learned I could carry over the excess into the next five years.

"This arrangement took away the worries I had about the land. What I did was to turn over the responsibility to others who are more able and will care for it on my behalf. Through this trust I satisfied my objectives to give to my church and other Christian institutions that I have supported for years. The trustee recently sold the land for $85,000. Assuming it cost $5,000 to sell the land, I will have $80,000 left and will receive 6½ percent from the trust.

5. I left $5,000 in the bank and placed $10,000 in a certificate of deposit at 7 percent interest. Income $700 a year.

6. The balance of my property, which included my stocks, bonds, and home, was placed in a revocable living trust. Each month I will receive an income check from the trustee.

7. Title to my home is to be given to my church by the trustee at my death. Since my home is across the street from the church, I thought it might be used in future expansion.

8. The $3,000 life insurance policy was given outright to the institution which helped me complete this plan.

"I will now receive a total income each year of nearly $16,000, including my social security payments. This is an increase of about $7,500 a year.

"What I like best about the revocable living trust is its flexibility. I can revoke it, amend it, withdraw from or add to the principal, change trustees, and do just about anything I want.

"We provided that if I should become disabled, the trustee will receive my income from all sources, pay my bills, and in effect take over complete management of my affairs.

"Once a person asked the question, 'What will happen if I wake up some morning and do not remember where my bank account and other property are?' This thought preyed on my mind for a long time. I found the trust to be my answer."

"When I die, the trustee will provide $200 a month life income for each of my aunts. He will arrange a gift annuity with the foreign mission agency for Constance, which will pay her $100 a month for life. The balance of my trust assets will be distributed in the following way: 5 percent to my local church; 20 percent to the college; and 75 percent to a foreign mission agency.

"I reduced the amount going to my church because I transferred title to my home to the church through the trust.

9. A new will was made that provided the same distribution as listed above.

"Now I understand my own financial plan. Instead of letting my property use me, sapping my energies with worry, I am using my money freely for my interests. I have someone to take over for me when I am unable to care for myself. I know my property will be distributed according to my wishes when I die and with the least cost to my estate.

"I was able to give more than I had ever imagined.

"For the first time in my life, I can see the whole financial picture. I am now using my assets to good advantage."

This is an example of how one person planned carefully for her future.

The type B planned giving officer equips himself to handle just this type of situation, and every institution has donors with similar needs. The estate planning approach, used along with the services of competent lawyers, trust officers, and others, is the ideal professional way to help people give.

Summary

In brief, here is how the estate planning process works with an individual.

The information needed for estate planning can be secured through the four "Ps" approach. By the four "Ps" I mean the *persons* in the donor's life, their use of the *properties* he owns, his *plans* for the persons in his life and the property he owns, and the *planners* who will help him complete his plans.

As far as the *persons* are concerned, it must be determined what persons or other institutions (besides yours) the donor wants to remember. You should ask about his responsibilities toward family members, relatives, friends, charitable institutions, and anyone else that he might wish to care for after his death. Remember to consider the emotional as well as the financial aspects.

In fact, his responsibility or desire to care for these people or institutions should be taken into account both for his remaining years of life as well as after his death. Estate planning actually involves planning to live as well as planning for death.

By *properties* we simply mean everything in which the person has a right of ownership. These properties should be listed as to whether or not they are held solely in the person's name, whether or not they are jointly held either with rights of survivorship or as tenants in common, whether or not there are trusts that have already been created, whether or not there are life insurance policies held, or whether or not there are other types of contracts that might validly pass property at the owner's death. Miscellaneous property and powers of appointment should be carefully reviewed, for they are often overlooked. It is also important to list the cost basis of the property and the income it produces.

The person's *plans* are really the meat of the process as he looks at the persons and the properties and then determines how he is going to conserve and eventually distribute these properties to the people in the proper proportions. Estate planning takes on a different light for each individual. For some people estate planning is a very easy task. For other people, even though the estates might be smaller, estate planning can be a very complicated process. Special situations may be evident where the estate might be best divided among the children equally; others will require unequal distribution. Look for potential planned giving arrangements to do the job, such as plans that will provide an income to specific beneficiaries.

By *planners*, I am referring to the members of the estate planning team. This team consists of the attorney, the trust officer, the CPA, and the chartered life underwriter. As a matter of practicality, many times all of these people will not actually come together to work out an individual's estate plan. It depends somewhat on the size of his estate and what the individual's objectives are. However, in many estates, particularly those that might be comprised of large and complex assets, all of the planners will be involved for one reason or another.

The *attorney* is the individual who is responsible for seeing that the estate plan is implemented. He must draft all of the legal documents. He should be included when the planning begins.

The trust officer will obviously be involved if there is either a trust in effect or if there is to be a trust or trusts included in the will.

The certified public accountant, the man responsible for handling the accounting of all the finances of the person, should be involved so that he can analyze the financial aspects, including tax consequences of the plan as they relate to the person's wishes.

The chartered life underwriter is qualified in the field of life insurance and will pay particular attention to the liquidity needs in estates. People who have large estates must be concerned about federal estate taxes and state death taxes, and they should provide the liquidity in their estates that will keep their heirs or executor from having to sell any of the assets of the estate at less than its full fair market value. Unfortunately, this type of sale is not uncommon.

The federal estate tax return is due nine months after the decedent's death, and often real estate, a business, or some other hard-to-sell asset must be sold within that period of time to pay these taxes. Such a forced sale means the executor cannot get as much for the property as he normally would.

If your donors are satisfied with their contact with you, they will sometimes suggest other prospects. I remember the time I visited with a woman who had arranged a gift annuity with the institution I represented. As I left, she said, "You should contact Mrs. S. She has much more money than I have, and she is very interested in your work."

I then asked her if she would call Mrs. S, tell her about me, and ask if I might stop in for a visit. She did, and the visit resulted in a deferred gift that was four times larger than the first woman's gift. Both of these women have now made careful plans for their estates.

Chapter Sixteen
Is Your Institution
Accountable?

Accountability has become a major concern for donors and institutions alike. Giving in America increases each year and the givers are asking more questions.

How much should we tell about our institutions? Does the donor have a right to know? Will our donors quit giving if they learn we have an endowment? These and other important questions are being asked by the management of many institutions.

About ten years ago, a donor I worked with was seeking information before he gave. We will call him "Mr. Robinson." I introduced this story early in the book—now here are the important details.

Mr. Robinson said, "I've inherited $5 million and I want to give much of it away. How can I learn more about the inner workings of these institutions? I want to be responsible in my giving."

For the last two decades I have visited with hundreds of people about giving. Mr. Robinson was the most conscientious and inspiring. Here is the story of how he gave to the right institutions—after investigation.

His father left a large estate to his mother, and Mr. Robinson was to get what was left at her death. She lived into her nineties, and at that time he was in his fifties.

Being a committed Christian, he had always given a good

part of his modest income to well-known Christian institutions. Now he had thrust upon him what he considered a sacred trust of these funds. He wanted to give wisely.

Together we devised a questionnaire that we first sent to thirteen institutions, then later to four others, keeping him anonymous. Here are the questions. Could your institution supply the requested information listed below? *Would* it?

1. Legal name.

2. Copy of bylaws and articles of incorporation.

3. Letter of tax-exemption.

4. Last audited balance sheet. Include all investments at cost and fair market value. (Is your annuity account separate? How much are the assets? Cost? Market? How much are your actuarial liabilities to annuitants? Are your annuity reserves free from the claims of general creditors?)

5. Statement of investment policy for reserve funds, annuities, endowments, etc.

6. How would you use $50,000 to $100,000 if received this year, next year, and the year after that?

7. What do you believe will be accomplished if money is given? What will be lost if not given?

8. What is your board of trustees' plan for obtaining financial support? Is it in writing?

9. Is the list of salaries, allowances, and expenses current?

10. Write a history of the organization of not more than two pages. Emphasize activities during the last three years.

11. What is distinctive about your organization? What is special about your goals in the current year?

12. How is your work carried on? What are your methods: evangelism, street preaching, tribal work, seminaries, radio? Explain in detail. How are workers selected for certain locations?

13. What percent of your income for the last year came from individuals, churches, corporations, foundations, legacies, other?

14. (If an educational institution), how much does it cost a student to go to school—including food, shelter, tuition, and

fees? Or (if a mission board) what is the average annual cost of keeping a missionary on the field or on furlough? (Total expenditure divided by the number of missionaries.) Do you charge a part of home office overhead for each missionary on the field?

15. How many people are working in this organization full-time? Part-time?

16. Doctrinal statement.

17. Is the organization controlled by board of reference or board of directors? How are they elected and by whom?

18. How do you encourage the pursuit of excellence on the part of your employees, students, or missionaries?

19. How do you measure the results achieved? Cite examples.

20. What is being done to train the management personnel of your organization to be current in both method and procedure?

21. In the event of dissolution of your organization, what happens to any assets in your organization? Be specific.

22. Who makes ultimate decisions on personnel dismissal or expansion of ministry? How do you select personnel?

Ten of the thirteen Christian institutions answered all the questions. Three refused on the basis that they didn't know who would be getting the information. (What difference did it make?) One executive even said he "didn't feel it was God's will" to furnish this information.

Mr. Robinson gave the ten institutions answering the questions about $30,000 each. He was, of course, disappointed that the three worthy institutions with highly effective missions felt they could not release financial information and policy statements. He said, "Since a charitable institution pays no taxes and exists at the pleasure of the public, it should have no information which cannot be released even to its worst enemy."

One other question, by the way, which should be added to the list today is: "What does it cost your organization to receive a gift dollar?"

Planning an Annual Report

An annual report to donors is an excellent way to convey to them that you have an "open door" policy. In fact, the report can be in simple form and made available to anyone on request. This is the best kind of disclosure, and whether or not a person writes for a copy, the fact that it is available has built in his mind a positive image of your institution. The public relations value is well worth the cost.

This type of report reinforces the confidence your givers have in your institution by showing them in brief form just what their gifts have accomplished during the past year. It is an opportunity to say "thank you," words that never wear out.

An annual report should *not* conjure up the image of a sophisticated prospectus, replete with profits and losses, or reflecting accelerated depreciation and investment credit. But rather, it should be an attractive and comprehensive—yet concise—report of your annual activities and what role your donors played in making these activities possible. A simple financial statement can be included showing basic income and expenditures. A more detailed report can be offered on request.

The report can also include specific projects that need to be funded, tell about the completion of certain programs, and even outline the giving opportunities—including planned giving options.

Chapter Seventeen
Taxes and Giving

By Philip Ray Converse, LL.B.

Philip Ray Converse is executive vice-president of Robert F. Sharpe & Co., Inc., Memphis, Tennessee, and is associate director of the National Planned Giving Institute. After graduating from Millsaps College and Jackson School of Law, both in Jackson, Mississippi, he became the assistant director of development and estate planning at Millsaps College.

In 1969 he moved to Knoxville, Tennessee, to become director of estate planning and deferred giving for the University of Tennessee system (five campuses). Mr. Converse was named by the United States Jaycees as one of the outstanding young men in America in 1972, the year he joined Robert F. Sharpe & Co., Inc.

He is a member of the Mississippi, Tennessee, and American Bar Associations. He is coauthor of a workbook, "The Guide to the Administration of Charitable Trusts Under the 1969 Tax Reform Act," which is published by the Council for the Advancement and Support of Education. He is a frequent speaker at meetings of regional and national groups on the subjects of taxation and planned giving, and he is the author of numerous articles and brochures on various plans of giving and their tax consequences.

Since the inception of the income, gift, and estate tax laws, Congress has always favored individuals supporting their favorite philanthropic institutions. This was most recently apparent in the 1969 Tax Reform Act when Congress, for the first time, made provisions that now allow individuals to deduct up to 50 percent of their contribution base for charitable gifts of certain types of property.[1]

With the 1969 act came other changes in the deductions that people could take for charitable giving. To understand the full effects of taxation and charitable giving, it is necessary to discuss the different types of charitable institutions that exist, the types of property that may be given to them, and the types of deductions that individuals can take.

Two Types of Institutions

For deduction purposes, charitable institutions are divided into two categories: 20 percent institutions and the 50 percent institutions. These categories are so named because charities that fit into the 50 percent category qualify for the 50 percent charitable deduction. Included in this category are schools, hospitals, churches, church-related organizations, universities, and certain medical research foundations.

The 20 percent group consists of private foundations. The distinguishing feature is that when an individual makes a gift to a qualified charitable institution (a 50 percent institution), as a general rule that individual may deduct the value of that gift to the extent that it does not exceed 50 percent of one's contribution base (adjusted gross income) computed without regard to any net operating loss carry back. In addition the individual may take advantage of the five-year carry-over rule, which states that any deductions that cannot be taken in the year of the gift (because of the limitations in any one year) can be carried forward to as many as five successive tax years.[2]

On the other hand, when a gift is made to a private foundation (a 20 percent institution), an individual can take the value of that gift to the extent that it doesn't exceed 20 percent of his adjusted gross income, and the five year carry-over provision is not allowed. For the purposes of discussion, we'll assume that

1. IRC Sec 170(b).
2. IRC Sec. 170(d)(1)(A).

189

for the next few paragraphs the gifts being made by donors are to the qualified or 50 percent charitable institutions.

Types of Property That Can Be Given

Cash

A cash gift is deductible for the face amount of the cash given. The donor may deduct the value of the cash to the extent that it doesn't exceed 50 percent of his adjusted gross income. If the gift does exceed 50 percent of his adjusted gross income, he may utilize the five-year carry-over provision.

EXAMPLE: Mr. Jones has an adjusted gross income of $20,000. He makes a gift of $12,000 to "X" institution. Mr. Jones can deduct $10,000 of his $12,000 gift in that year and carry forward $2,000 into the following tax year.

Gifts of Ordinary Income Property

Certain gifts of so-called ordinary income property are treated differently from cash gifts. This property includes that which, if sold by the taxpayer, would generate ordinary income.

Included in this type of property are inventory items of a businessman, works of art created by the donor, manuscripts, memorandums prepared by or for the donor, and any capital asset held for less than one year. Gifts of ordinary income property may only be deducted to the extent of their cost basis.[3]

EXAMPLE: Mr. Smith operates a sole proprietorship and has a certain inventory item that cost him $400. The retail value of that same item is $800. If Mr. Jones makes a gift of the inventory item to a qualified charitable institution, his tax deduction will not be for the full $800, but rather only for the $400 base cost. Mr. Jones can deduct that $400 to the extent that it doesn't exceed 50 percent of his adjusted gross income.

Donors should be aware of the fact that if they make gifts of capital assets, which have been held for less than a period of one

---

3. IRC Sec. 170(e)(1)(A).

year, their charitable deduction will be limited to cost basis only.

EXAMPLE: Mrs. Fellow purchased certain securities for $500 in January of 1977. In August of 1977, these same securities were worth $2,000. Mrs. Fellow made a gift to her favorite charitable institution. As a result she can take as a charitable tax deduction only the $500 cost basis.

Please note, also, that effective January 1, 1978, in order for a capital asset to qualify for long-term capital gains treatment, the asset must have been held for a period of at least one year.

Gifts of Art

In exploring gifts of ordinary income, perhaps the greatest inequity in the 1969 act relates to artists who are interested in making gifts of their own art work to charitable institutions. Since this is considered an ordinary income item, a gift of this type will only qualify for a cost basis deduction. In other words, an artist making a contribution of a very valuable painting that he had painted could only deduct as a charitable gift the value of his canvas, paint, brushes, etc.

Certain gifts of tangible personal property, which are not in the hands of the creator himself, receive other treatment as far as the law is concerned. When making a gift of tangible personal property, a donor must consider what type of charitable institution the gift is being made to, and in fact, what the charitable institution plans to do with the property once it receives it. The law now says that if a donor makes a gift to an "unrelated" charitable organization his charitable deduction for tax purposes must be reduced by one-half the value of the appreciation.[4] As to whether or not a gift is related or unrelated, each set of circumstances must be taken into consideration.

EXAMPLE: Mr. Brown purchased a painting from an artist for $1,000. Now three years later that same painting is worth $2,000. Mr. Brown has decided to make a gift of the painting to a hospital, which plans to sell the painting. Because this is

4. IRC Sec. 170(e)(1)(B)(i).

considered as an unrelated gift by the Internal Revenue Service, Mr. Brown's deduction will be limited to his cost basis of $1,000, plus one-half of the appreciation for a total gift of $1,500. On the other hand, if Mr. Brown were to make a gift of that same painting to a museum whose tax-exempt purpose is the displaying of paintings of that type, then his charitable deduction would be for the full market value of the painting on the date the gift was made. In other words, the entire $2,000 would be allowed as a charitable contribution deduction.

In the first example, the $1,500 deductible gift could be taken to the extent that it didn't exceed 50 percent of Mr. Brown's adjusted gross income, since it is a gift of ordinary income property.

On the other hand, in the second example, the $2,000 charitable contribution deduction can only be deducted to the extent that it does not exceed 30 percent of Mr. Brown's adjusted gross income. In either case, the five-year carry-over provision does apply.

The regulations do point out that if a painting is contributed to an educational institution and that institution uses the painting for educational purposes by placing it in a library for display, or hangs it elsewhere to be used by art students for study purposes, then the use will be a related one. But if the painting were sold by the institution and the proceeds used, then the gift would be considered unrelated.

In order to substantiate a deduction of tangible personal property for related use, a donor must either: (1) Establish that the property is *not* put to an unrelated use by the donee, or (2) show that it is reasonable to anticipate at the time of contribution that the property will not be put to an unrelated use by the donee.

Gifts of Appreciated Property

There are other potential gifts for which a reduction must be made in considering the total value of the tax deductible gift. For example, if a donor makes a contribution subject to a liability accepted by the institution, he must reduce the fair market value of the gift by the amount of the liability.

This naturally leads us into a discussion of the tax deductions allowed for gifts of long-term capital gain property. In order for an asset to qualify, it must have been held by the donor for a period of one year or longer. When a donor makes a gift of long term appreciated property to a qualified charitable institution, the deduction will be for the full fair market value of the property at the time of the gift and can be taken to the extent that it doesn't exceed 30 percent of the donor's adjusted gross income.[5] The five-year, carry-over provision applies.

EXAMPLE: Mr. Goodwin acquired certain securities in June of 1976 for $750. In June of 1978, these securities are worth $2,000. Upon making a gift of the securities, Mr. Goodwin is allowed a charitable deduction of the full fair market value, or $2,000, which can be taken to the extent that it doesn't exceed 30 percent of his adjusted gross income. In addition to the charitable income tax deduction, the donor will avoid all of the capital gains taxes by making the gift to the charitable institution. This is always the case except for charitable gift annuities and bargain sales, which are discussed later in this chapter.

A bargain sale results from a donor's "selling" property to a charitable institution for an amount less than its fair market value. This generates a charitable income tax deduction for the difference between the price received by the donor from the institution and the fair market value of the property at the time of the sale. However, when a bargain sale takes place the donor must report some of the capital gain.[6] This has precluded the very favorable treatment that bargain sales received prior to the 1969 Tax Reform Act. (The donor then received not only a charitable deduction for the gift portion, but also avoided the capital gains tax when selling appreciated property to a charitable institution.)

There are other situations that will trigger the bargain sales rules, such as a contribution of long-term appreciated property subject to an indebtedness, or funding a charitable gift annuity with long-term appreciated property, or a contribution of

5. IRC Sec. 170(b)(1)(D).
6. IRC Sec. 170(e)(2) and IRC 1011(b).

depreciable property in which the depreciation must be recaptured.

Retaining an Interest

There are many ways by which a donor can make a gift to his favorite charitable institution and retain some type of interest during his lifetime. Now for a discussion of these types of gifts:

Charitable Gift Annuities

A charitable gift annuity is a contract whereby a donor transfers cash, securities, or other assets (not tangible personal property) to a qualified charitable institution. In exchange for those assets the qualified charity agrees to pay the donor or some other designated beneficiary(ies) a fixed income for life.

Because the donor has made an irrevocable gift, he is entitled to a charitable income tax deduction for a portion of the amount of money or assets transferred in exchange for the fixed payment for life.[7] The gift portion or the amount of the deduction is determined by using the rates adopted by the institution and certain treasury tables that take into consideration the life expectancy of the annuitants and presumed earnings of the annuity. The charitable institution backs up the income payments to the beneficiaries with all of the assets of the institution.

In addition to the initial income tax deduction, a portion of the money returned to the beneficiary represents tax-free income.

If the gift annuity is funded with long-term appreciated property, the donor is deemed to have made a bargain sale when funding the gift annuity. As such, a portion of the appreciation must be taxed to the donor as a capital gain. However, there is a provision in the law allowing the donor to spread the capital gain over his life expectancy provided that the gift annuity is not assignable, and provided that the donor is one of the annuitants.[8]

7. IRC Reg. 1.170 A-1(d)(1).
8. IRC Reg. 1.170 A-1(d)(3); IRC Reg. 1.011-2 and IRC Reg. 1.011-2(a)(4)(ii).

Another type of gift annuity is the deferred payment gift annuity. The same gift annuity concepts apply with the exception that when a donor funds the annuity he designates his income payments to be made at some later time in life. To qualify as a deferred payment gift annuity, payments must begin at least one year after the gift is funded. For people in high income brackets, the deferred payment gift annuity is something that should be considered. The charitable income tax deduction is allowed at the time the gift is made and not at the time the payments begin. Thus, it is possible for a donor to offset some high income during peak earning years and defer payments until later when earnings normally won't be so high.

In addition, when payments begin, a portion will be considered a tax-free distribution of principal and thus nontaxable. If the deferred payment gift annuity is funded with appreciated property, the donor incurs some capital gains tax because of the bargain sale rules, but none of the capital gains tax will be due until the actual income payments begin to the donor.

Charitable Remainder Trusts.

The 1969 Tax Reform Act brought into being two new types of charitable remainder trusts heretofore unknown in the charitable giving field. These are the charitable remainder annuity trust and the charitable remainder unitrust.[9]

A *charitable remainder annuity trust* is created by a donor transferring cash, securities, or other assets to a trustee in exchange for the trustee's promise to pay a fixed sum of money to named beneficiaries, said amount not to be less than 5 percent of the initial fair market value of the trust assets. This income must be paid for either the lives of the beneficiaries or a fixed number of years which shall not be more than twenty years. At the death of the last beneficiary or at the expiration of the term of years the trust will terminate and the assets will be distributed to the charitable institution. The charitable remain-

9. IRC Sec. 664.

der annuity trust may be written for more than 5 percent, but in no event can it ever be for less than 5 percent.[10]

EXAMPLE: Mr. Jones transfers $100,000 of appreciated securities to fund a charitable remainder annuity trust. The trustee holds the funds for the eventual distribution to a qualified charitable institution, and, in the meantime, according to the terms of the trust agreement, pays Mr. Jones a fixed amount of $6,000 per year. This would represent a 6 percent charitable remainder annuity trust.

The charitable remainder annuity trust, by its definition, is a tax-exempt trust, and a gift to fund an annuity trust is an irrevocable gift. The donor retains no right in the trust other than the right to receive the income. By law, the payments from an annuity trust must be made at least on an annual basis. The beneficiaries designated to receive the trust income must be living at the time the annuity is created. When funding a charitable remainder annuity trust, a donor is entitled to a charitable income tax deduction based on the present value of the remainder interest.[11] The remainder interest is that amount which can be determined as the organization of the trust's assets based on certain assumptions, such as the donor's life expectancy, the trust's presumed rate of earnings, pay out, etc. This can be calculated through the use of treasury tables and the deduction is available in the year in which the donor establishes the trust.

In addition to the income tax deduction, when appreciated securities or property is used to fund an annuity trust, the donor avoids all of the capital gains taxes. Income paid to a beneficiary from an annuity trust is taxed according to a tier structure that runs as follows:

- First, as ordinary income to the extent of the trust's ordinary income for the current taxable year and then any undistributed ordinary income earned from prior years.
- Capital gain to the extent of the trust's capital gains

10. IRC Reg. 1.664-2(a)(2).
11. IRC Sec. 664(e).

earned in the current year and then all the undistributed capital gains earned from prior years.

• "Other income," which basically will be income from tax-exempt securities.

• Corpus, or principal, which is a distribution of the trust assets themselves.

Under the annuity trust rules, if the income earned from the trust in the taxable year is insufficient to meet the required pay-out provisions, then the trust must by law invade corpus, but corpus can only be invaded for purposes of making income payments to the donor.

If a donor funds a charitable remainder annuity trust and is the only recipient of the income, then at the time of his death, the value of the trust assets will be included in the estate but will "wash out" as a charitable estate tax deduction. If the donor has a survivor to receive income upon his death, then the charitable estate tax deduction will be for the present value of the remainder interest determined by using the survivor's age at the time of the donor's death.

The *charitable remainder unitrust* is created by a donor's transferring securities or other assets to a trustee in exchange for the trustee's promise to pay an income that is equal to at least 5 percent of the net fair market value of the trust assets as determined annually. The trust will terminate at the death of the last of the beneficiaries, and all of the corpus and accrued income will be distributed to the named charitable institution.

As we saw in the annuity trust, when funding a charitable remainder unitrust a donor is entitled to a charitable income tax deduction for the present value of the remainder interest.[12] In addition, if the trust is funded with appreciated property, then the donor avoids the capital gains taxes. The charitable estate tax deductions work the same way as discussed in the annuity trust above.

The unitrust may be written for a percentage that is greater than 5 percent, but in no instance may it ever be written with a

12. IRC Sec. 664(e).

percentage of less than 5 percent. One chief difference between the annuity trust and the unitrust is the fact that a donor or another person may make an additional contribution to an existing unitrust. Additional contributions are prohibited as far as an annuity trust is concerned. Obviously, a donor will choose either an annuity trust or a unitrust depending on what his needs are. The annuity trust provides for a fixed income distribution, whereas the unitrust provides for a variable income distribution.

Two Alternatives to Unitrust

In addition to the regular unitrust, which is most often referred to as a straight unitrust, the provisions of the code allow for two alternative versions of the charitable remainder unitrust. They are now commonly referred to as the *net income unitrust* and the *net income plus make-up unitrust*.

The *net income unitrust* allows the trustee to include a provision that the amount of income distributed each year to the beneficiaries will be the lesser of the percentage stipulated in the trust multiplied by the fair market value of the assets determined annually, or the actual income earned.

The *net income plus make-up unitrust* has an additional provision to the net income unitrust, which says that in years in which the trust earns more than the stated percentage multiplied by the fair market value, that the trustee can make up any accumulated deficiencies incurred in prior years.

Pooled Income Fund

Section 642(c)(5) of the Internal Revenue Code defines a pooled income fund trust. The pooled income fund as a trust was a product of the 1969 Tax Reform Act and allows many donors to contribute to a common trust fund for the purposes of eventually aiding a charitable institution. To have a qualified pooled income fund, each donor making a contribution must retain for himself for life an income interest in the property transferred to such fund or must create an income interest for other designated beneficiaries. By law, the trustee must commingle all of the gifts received with other donors' gifts to the fund and must, at least annually, make a distribution of the income earned by the fund to the beneficiaries based on their pro-rata share of the fund.

At the death of each life income beneficiary, his portion of the fund is severed and transferred to the charitable institution.

EXAMPLE: "Y" College creates a pooled income fund. It determines that each initial unit of the fund will be worth $100. Donor A contributes $10,000 to the fund, thus he has participation to the extent of 100 units. Depending on how many other donors join the fund and what the earnings of the fund are for that year, Donor A will receive an income distribution based on his 100 units. At the time of Donor A's death, his 100 units will be severed from the fund and transferred directly to the charitable institution. When making a gift to a pooled income fund, a donor is entitled to a charitable income tax deduction based on the present value of the remainder interest in the fund.[13] The deduction is available in the year the gift is made and can be taken to the extent that it does not exceed either 50 percent or 30 percent of the donor's contribution base, depending on what type of property is given to the fund.

If the donor uses long-term appreciated property to fund the pooled income fund, he will avoid all of the capital gains tax. If a donor contributes to a pooled income fund and is the only life income beneficiary, then at the time of his death his estate will have a "wash out," which means that his share of the fund will incur no estate taxes. If there is a survivor to the donor, the estate tax deduction is allowed for the present value of the remainder interest determined by utilizing the survivor's age at the time of the donor's death.

Life Estate Contracts

A person may make a gift of a personal residence or family farm, retaining the use of the property during his lifetime. The "remainder interest" becomes a gift to the charity at the death of the donor. If the property is transferred irrevocably to the charity, with the life estate provision, the donor is allowed a

13. IRC Sec. 642(c)(5).

current tax deduction, but this applies only to property that is considered a "personal residence" or to a family farm.

The donor's income tax deduction is based on the fair market value of the property reduced by the depreciation computed on a straight line basis. Only homes or improvements on land must be considered as depreciable items and not the land itself. After depreciation has been considered, the remaining value must be reduced to the present value of the charitable remainder interest.

The regulations exclude, for charitable deduction purposes, property that is not being used for the production of agricultural products or in use for raising certain livestock; or if a residence, it must be one that is used by the donor as a personal residence. The regulations specifically outline provisions which allow condominiums to qualify as personal residences presuming that they are actually being used for that purpose.

Chapter Eighteen
Off and Running

Now you have a host of information on the subject of planned giving. What should you do first? What can you do now?

How to Begin Your Planned Giving Program

Step 1. Get Proper Authorization

When you start a planned gifts program in your institution, the first step is to seek approval of the board of trustees to commence the program. Your attorney could prepare a suitable resolution such as the following to be presented to them.

> *Resolved, the   (Board)   authorizes the establishment of a planned gifts program for the purpose of encouraging gifts of securities, land, life insurance, bequests, and other special gifts from its membership.*

Step 2. Appoint a Director

The next step is to appoint one person to direct the program. The type of person to place in this position will depend on the particular institution. The person should be able to manage the institution's total planned giving effort.

Most institutions will be able to afford a full-time person. But the next best approach is to employ a person on a part-time basis. Some institutions hire a retired business executive to look after this part of the financial development work.

An unpaid volunteer is sometimes suggested but there is little history of success in this approach.

Step 3. Establish an Advisory Committee

This committee should be made up of friends of the institution who are lawyers, CPAs, life underwriters, trust officers, and stockbrokers. The purpose of this committee is to advise, encourage, and support the person in charge of the program.

Step 4. Begin a Wills Emphasis Program

See page 103 (and following) for steps to starting your bequest program. And as you do, you may be encouraged to remember your job is not a new idea. These ancient words of wisdom were penned almost twenty centuries ago:

> Instruct those who are rich in this world's goods . . . to be ready to give away and to share, and so acquire a treasure which will form a good foundation for the future. . . .
>
> 1 Timothy 6:17-19*

---

*From *The New English Bible.* © The Delegates of the Oxford University Press and the Syndics of the Cambridge University Press 1961, 1970. Reprinted by permission.

Appendix One
What the Banquet
Approach Can Do for
Your Organization

The banquet approach to donor relations is widely used by many institutions. For the most part, banquets are used to secure cash and pledges, to fund the annual budget, or to secure money for special projects.

The thrust of this chapter will be to show how to organize successful banquets. To do this, we will examine the approaches used by two institutions.

Institution A

The first step is to list those to be invited to the banquet. Generally these people are currently giving to Institution A. The institution sends invitations to all donors and includes an R.S.V.P. date. Those who don't respond to the letter are telephoned.

The management of Institution A selects a banquet committee from the group that responds affirmatively to the invitation. Every couple on the committee is assigned to a table for ten persons and is asked to invite eight other people who are not familiar with the work of Institution A.

The banquet committee (under the direction of the institution's management) then undertakes to contact all those planning to attend as well as any donors who can definitely not attend the banquet. A few local foundations might also be added to the list of those to be contacted. The objectives to be obtained by personal contact at this stage are two-fold: (1) to find one or more donors or foundations who will pay for the banquet (otherwise, the banquet expense is borne by Institution A), and (2) to secure the larger pledges prior to the night of the banquet.

For example, suppose your banquet goal is $75,000. You might have one gift of $10,000, one of $5,000, three gifts of $2,500 each, and a hundred gifts ranging from $100 to $1,000. The total amount received prior to the banquet would then amount to approximately $50,000. The night of the banquet, you are then seeking only $25,000 in small gifts and pledges. This approach may sound easy as you read about it, but it isn't. In order to reach this goal, a large amount of time will be spent in researching and contacting key people. The desired result does not just happen. In order to achieve prior gifts and pledges equal to two-thirds of the goal, someone must make it happen.

On the night of the banquet, the chairman of the banquet committee tells those in attendance that the banquet has been paid for by friends of Institution A. The donor or donors may wish to remain anonymous. When it is time to seek pledges, it is wise to mention the total previously pledged by "insiders."

In support of the banquet approach, a contact program is developed using quarterly letters and newsletters to collect pledges, to seek gifts from others, to report on the progress of Institution A's work, and to simply say "thank you."

The overall budget of Institution A is several hundred thousand each year. The banquet is just one way to "raise" friends and secure gifts.

A Case History

I have asked Rod Sargent, vice-president for development of the Navigators, to tell how his organization got started with fund raising banquets and how the banquets have worked for them across the nation.

About two years ago I was asked by our Florida state director if I could help his staff of eight men bring their monthly income up to budget. As is true in many Christian organizations, an oddity permeated the thinking of some of these men. They assumed that if they concentrated on their ministries of helping people spiritually, adequate income would automatically follow. Their philosophy was—if income is low, don't go about asking for money. Instead, intensify your ministry efforts, or pray and trust God for it, but don't come right out and ask for money.

My first objective was to persuade these men that soliciting contributions is biblical, could be handled inoffensively, and would help them reach their financial objectives.

After discussing various methods of fund raising, we decided to experiment with a fund raising banquet. This banquet would be held within the state of Florida where we had an active outreach. If this first banquet succeeded, additional banquets would be planned.

Our first effort focused on gathering information about fund raising banquets. I visited several institutions that used banquets extensively. Each of them freely shared its philosophy of banquet fund-raising, what to do, and what not to do. Two organizations gave me copies of their banquet manuals with step-by-step instructions on how to have a successful banquet.

From these resource materials, I extracted that which I felt would be appropriate to our organization and presented a plan to our Florida staff.

Our first step was to form a banquet committee. We felt it would be helpful to invite business people from the community who could advise us on a variety of issues, such as avoiding banquet dates that would conflict with other activities planned within the community. The committee we formed was composed of six professional people from the area plus three of our staff members. The criteria for actually selecting these people were that (1) they were to be knowledgeable and enthusiastic about our organization; (2) they were to be influential in the community so that they could be effective in generating interest among their peers in attending the banquet; and (3) they had to be willing and able to give time and money to help insure a successful banquet.

After forming the banquet committee, we involved them in the decision-making process on the following issues:

• They decided whether or not a fund raising banquet would be held in their city. This was actually a backwards step, but we felt it was beneficial to involve them in this decision. By doing so, the banquet became *their* decision and not simply a project handed down to them. Most people work harder to achieve goals they themselves have helped to establish.

• We involved them in the selection of the banquet facility. Our recommendation to the committee was to select a first-class facility, the kind of place that might evoke a response like, "Oh, great, I have always wanted to go there," or "I have been there and the food is fabulous." At first, several committee members argued that Christian organizations should hold their banquets in less pretentious places. We checked out the place they recommended and found the facilities to be rather ordinary, and the reputation for food and service was only average, not outstanding. We also discovered that the cost of having the banquet at the finer facility was not that much more than at the second-rate place. We chose the first-class facility.

• We discussed how to fund the banquet expenses. Would we sell tickets to those attending the banquet; would we try to presubscribe the cost of the banquet; or would we pay the expenses from the money raised the night of the banquet? The decision was made that all banquet guests would be invited to come as our guests.

• When it came to the program, the committee wanted a well-known speaker, someone whose reputation would attract people to the banquet. I opposed this idea, feeling it would be preferable to feature our organization rather than a personality. If we were going to have numerous banquets around the country, getting a well-known speaker for each program would be difficult and increase expenses.

The preference of the committee, however, was to invite a

well-known speaker. Comparing the results of the first banquet with over forty banquets held since that time, the results in terms of funds raised and attendance were no better in cases where the well-known speakers were used.

For promotion, we began with the fact that there were approximately four hundred people on our mailing list within a fifty-mile radius of the city. Forty-five percent of these had made a gift within the past twenty-four months. All donors were called and thanked for their giving. They were told about the fund raising banquet and asked to attend the banquet and to bring some friends. They were told they were being invited as our guests and were then informed that within a few days they would receive a letter of invitation with all the details and a reply card.

We learned that a volunteer equipped with calling instructions and phone numbers could easily handle thirty to forty calls on a Saturday morning. Calling between 9:00 A.M. and noon is an excellent time to find people at home. Invitations were mailed to arrive within a week of the telephone call. A reply card with the local address of the reservations secretary was included. The reservations secretary had been provided with a printed acknowledgment letter and banquet tickets, which she mailed to all who sent in reservation cards.

Ten days before the banquet, we telephoned everyone on the mailing list, both donors and nondonors, from whom we had not heard. This second telephone effort is always productive in that invariably it more than doubles the number of reservations received through the mail.

Here is a summary of the results of the first banquet:

1. Attendance totaled 340 people. Registrations prior to the banquet had totaled 377. As a rule of thumb, a 10 percent deduction from the total number of reservations gives a very accurate figure on the number who will actually attend the banquet.

2. Pledges totaled $26,372, cash contributions came to $2,495, for a total amount raised of $28,867.

3. Of those attending the banquet, 40 percent had not previously attended a Navigator function.

4. Fifty-nine percent of these new contacts became donors giving us a total of seventy-nine new donors.

5. The new donors gave $9,850, approximately one third of the total raised.

6. Forty percent of all those attending responded with pledges or contributions for a total of 134 responses.

7. Pledges and contributions from the banquet represented a 34 percent increase in gift income for the staff in that city.

Since this first banquet, forty-eight banquets have been conducted, and we have raised a total in cash and pledges of $810,000. Banquet expenses have run between 20 and 30 percent of the funds raised, depending on the city, the banquet facility, the menu, etc. The total number of persons who have attended the forty-eight banquets is 16,130. Forty percent of these were new prospects, and sixty percent have given gifts or filled out pledge cards. The number of new donors totals 3,600, and they have given $244,000.

I believe successful banquets are the result of careful planning, effective promotion, a stimulating program, and attention to detail. Allowing ample time for planning insures that all necessary tasks can be accomplished. We normally allow a minimum of three months for banquet preparations.

Some general thoughts and guidelines are as follows:

1. Members of the banquet committee serve various functions—for instance, the job of committee chairman is to assure that all tasks get accomplished. He also handles all arrangements with the banquet facility.

In selecting the banquet facility, the chairman must inspect it, talk with the salespeople, and look for signs of well or poorly managed facilities. Some red flags are worn carpets, unkept rest rooms and lounges, and incompetent help. A lack of accessibility and poor parking are strong negatives. I suggest eating in the coffee shop of a facility that may appear doubtful. Food quality and service will probably be about the same for the banquet. Facilities that are heavily booked can usually be depended upon for good food and fast service—*but not always*.

The committee chairman must also make arrangements with the banquet manager. This includes selecting the menu for the banquet. He should request that the salad and appetizer be preset in order to save time. Serving hot soup is often quite time consuming. A light but tasty dessert is preferable. The meal service can usually be completed within one to one-and-a-half hours. The banquet manager should be told that this type of service is necessary to keep the program moving and to end it on time.

2. The reservations secretary receives reservation cards sent in by those making banquet reservations. She then assigns guest seating and provides for an information table at the banquet. The purpose of the information table is to tell guests their table numbers if they have forgotten their tickets. Organizational brochures and various types of literature can also be distributed from the information table but preferably at the end of the banquet program.

3. Guests are assigned to tables. This requires that each table be numbered, but most facilities have numbers and stands for this purpose. When guests enter the banquet room and find a table that is theirs, it helps make them feel that they belong. This is a positive factor, especially for people who are new to the organization.

4. The telephone coordinator arranges for the initial calling of donors and for the follow-up calls that take place ten days prior to the banquet. This person must recruit the callers, instruct them, and make certain that all calls are completed.

5. The host and hostess coordinators must recruit a host and hostess for each table, provide instruction for them, and provide name tags and a felt tip pen for each table. Guests are asked to fill out their own name tags. Table host and hostesses are also provided with pledge cards and are instructed to pass them out when the speaker calls for them toward the end of his financial presentation.

6. Every program participant should be required to write out his presentation, rehearse it, and insure that it falls within the time limit given to him.

7. Before the banquet, check room arrangements and equipment. Is the podium located in the proper place? Is it lighted? Is it on risers? Have the screen and audio visuals been placed in their proper positions? Have they been tested? Has the sound system been checked out?

8. The proper kind of music, either instrumental or vocal, can enhance the program. By "proper," I'm referring to a standard of excellence. If the very finest musician or vocalist is not available, it is best not to include any music on the program.

9. Start the banquet promptly at 7:00 even if everyone has not yet arrived. After all the guests have been served dessert, and approximately fifteen minutes before the program is to begin, the master of ceremonies should announce that the program will begin in fifteen minutes and suggest that guests may wish to make a phone call, go to the restroom, or just get up and stretch their legs.

10. An excellent goal that will be appreciated by all the guests is to conclude the program by 9:30 if possible.

Another banquet to consider is an appreciation banquet (as opposed to a fund raising banquet) where you can bring people together for an enjoyable evening, provide quality entertainment, make a progress report on achievement within the organization, and heartily express appreciation for all who have done so much to make the work of your institution possible.

Appendix Two
Federal and State
Laws Regulating
Charitable Giving

by Philip Ray Converse, LL.B.

In recent years, federal, state and even local governments have become vitally interested in charitable organizations and the way in which they conduct their fund raising activities.

The interest on the part of each of these legislative bodies stems from the fact that in recent years there have been certain abuses by some charitable organizations in the way they have solicited, managed, and eventually distributed their funds.

Though most charitable organizations operate their programs in a prudent manner, history would hold it inevitable that when such a large number of organizations are involved in anything, there will be institutions among them that will intentionally or unwittingly fail to comply with all the laws or ethics set for the whole.

While most charitable organizations would serve as models (for which they receive their tax-exempt status), there are a few rotten apples in the barrel. Correction of abuses is usually much more difficult than setting forth initial guidelines, and the corrections often wind up as a myriad of difficult new laws to understand, adjust to, and, sometimes, even to comply with.

To appropriately identify some of the complexities that local, state, and federal regulations can bring to bear on charitable organizations, I have decided to attack the problem from several angles. Initially, the discussion will relate to an example of a local jurisdiction that is causing a great deal of concern to charitable organizations interested in pursuing their fund raising possibilities in a particular geographic area. That area is the city of Los Angeles.

Among other things, the Los Angeles Municipal Code, Ordinance Number 77,000, requires that before any charitable appeal can be made in that county, at least ten days prior to the inauguration of the solicitation campaign, or the solicitation for a dance show, entertainment, sale, concert, lecture or other special event designed to obtain funds for charitable uses, it is necessary to file with the city social services department a notice of intention to solicit. This notice must be signed by two officers of the soliciting organization.

Full information must be submitted to the department, which then evaluates the services to be performed and ascertains whether or not that fund raising activity is necessary. The information sent from the organization to the social services department must include copies of the articles of incorporation or constitution, the bylaws, roster of officers, auditor's financial statement, and a description of the charitable services provided.

Only after reviewing this information and issuing the charitable organization an information card, which contains the important facts for prospective donors to consider in determining the desirability of making a contribution to the organization, can any solicitation be done. During the solicitation, each solicitor must carry a reproduction of the information card issued and show it to all people solicited.

If the appeal is done by mail a facsimile of the information card must be enclosed with each appeal. Following the solicitation a report of the results showing receipts, expenditures, and the distribution of the net proceeds must be filed within thirty days of the termination of the fund raising campaign or the date of a special event.

Some of the specific language from the standards issued by the social services department reads as follows:

1. Fund raising costs for all direct appeals shall not exceed 20 percent of the total receipts.

2. A local organization must be established with a minimum eleven-member board.

3. Bylaws must be adopted spelling out the soliciting organization's name, purpose, procedures for management, and election of officers and their duties.

4. All local fund raising must be conducted under the responsibility and direction of the local organization.

5. All solicitation receipts must be deposited in a bank account set up in the name of the organization.

6. The local organization must conduct regular meetings to assure the stipulated level of local control.

If a charitable organization thinks it can circumvent this particular statute by using the mail, radio, or television, section 44.13 of the ordinance reads:

> That no person shall solicit any contributions by printed matter or published article, or over the radio, television, telephone or telegraph, unless such publicity shall contain the data and information required to be set forth on the information card.

It is evident from these rules that most organizations would simply have to forego any solicitation in Los Angeles.

As I mentioned earlier, regulation is not only taking place at the local level, there is also very active legislation at the state level, and more states are getting into the picture each year. Currently, at least thirty-one states (plus the District of Columbia) have some kind of legislation regulating the fund raising activities of charitable organizations.

This appendix contains an outline of the states that currently have laws regulating the solicitation of charitable gifts (see Table 11). I should warn that these laws change quite rapidly, and, in fact, it is not unknown that some laws put on the books have even been repealed while others are rewritten to correct deficiencies in prior laws.

To take a broad survey, we might look at several states to see how they regulate the solicitation of charitable gifts. Minnesota, for example, has a registration procedure with the secretary of state's office. In this state there is a limitation of 30 percent of the amount of money raised which can be given to professional fund raisers. The state requires that six months after the end of the calendar or fiscal year, there must be an annual report filed by the charitable organization.

The State of New York's registration procedure is done through the board of social welfare, and their cost limitations outline that no more than 50 percent of the mail solicitation may be spent on sending unordered merchandise. They require a financial report within six months of the close of the fiscal year.

North Carolina requires a licensing procedure with the department of human resources, and its law specifies that no more than 35 percent of the funds received from the public may be spent by the organization for solicitation and fund raising expenses.

On the other hand, some states like Oklahoma and Ohio, while requiring a registration procedure with the commissioner of charities and corrections and the attorney general, have no cost limitations on fund raising.

Another confusing thing about state statutes is that most states have some type of exemption (in regard to solicitation cost limits) for certain charitable organizations. For example, in the thirty-one states that have registration or licensing requirements, religious organizations—including churches and their affiliates—are normally exempt in virtually all of these states. Other states might also exempt educational institutions, museums, voluntary health and welfare agencies, etc.

A charitable organization planning to actively solicit either in its own state or outside of its state, whether by way of personal solicitation, mail, radio, or television, should be sure that it has checked with the licensing agent of that particular state in order to be fully registered.

In addition to local and state regulations of charitable gifts, the federal government apparently in the future might also begin this type of registration and licensing.

It is obvious that with thirty-one states having enacted thirty-one different laws with varying exemptions, registration and licensing procedures, limitations on fund raising costs, and requirements on filing dates for annual reports, it is very difficult for a nationwide charitable organization to keep all of these requirements straight. Thus, in recent years there has been much discussion on the possibility of establishing uniformity of some of these statutes through federal legislation. Even if this were to happen, complexities are readily apparent when all of the different types of organizations and their special fund raising situations are considered.

The Wilson Bill

The most actively considered piece of federal legislation on this topic today is the so-called "Wilson Bill." The Wilson Bill was most recently introduced on January 4, 1977. Without going into finite detail, a few of the things that the Wilson Bill would do are as follows:

It would apply to any charitable organization that solicits contributions through any means, including contributions through the mail. The Wilson Bill is primarily designed to allow a prospective donor the right to obtain full financial information on the organization to which he might contribute. Included in this kind of information would be such things as the legal name and principal business address of the charitable organization, the purpose for which the solicitation is being made, how the contributions are eventually to be used, and the percentage of funds being raised that would actually go to charitable use.

Obviously, this would mean that the organization would have to reveal what its fund raising and management costs were for the preceding fiscal year.

Probably the most controversial section of the bill is whether or not fund raising costs should be included at the point of solicitation, or whether an offer should simply be made to the prospective donor to provide the financial information on request. The Wilson Bill would require that the information be included at the time of the solicitation. Such information would have to be clearly outlined to the donor in a very conspicuous place and printed in legible type contrasting with the other printed matter in the solicitation.

Another key consideration is who would actually administer these provisions. Many representatives of charitable organizations feel that the idea of having the U.S. Postal Authority regulate this kind of charitable giving activity would be a terrible mistake. They feel it would be done much better by the U.S. Treasury.

Most of the laws we have discussed apply to the solicitation of outright gifts on behalf of charitable organizations. For those organizations in the field of planned giving that are actively seeking bequests, charitable gift annuities, charitable remainder trusts, and life estate contracts, there are other laws to be concerned with.

In recent years some states, in an effort to more closely supervise the activities of charitable organizations, have enacted specific legislation that refers directly to charitable gift annuities.

For example, New York, New Jersey, Florida, California, Oregon, Minnesota, and Wisconsin have enacted laws having specific requirements for charitable organizations interested in contacting residents. Fortunately, there is some degree of uniformity in these laws.

The key interest by states is obviously to make sure that residents who contribute funds for charitable gift annuities, in exchange for a promise to receive income, will actually receive that income. Thus, most of these states have requirements that cause the charitable organization to either reinsure its gift annuities with commercial insurance companies, or to set aside a reserve fund that in effect will guarantee gift annuity payments. As an example of one state's regulation of gift annuities, the following shows what an organization must submit in New Jersey to obtain a gift annuity permit.

Application For Special Annuity Permit By Charitable Religious, Missionary, Educational or Philanthropic Corporations or Associations (N.J.S. 17B:17-13.1)

To the Commissioner of Insurance of the State of New Jersey:
    The undersigned, the _____
_____ of _____ State of _____
being desirous of receiving gifts of money in the State of New Jersey conditioned upon or in return for its agreement to pay an annuity to the donor or his nominee, hereby makes application for a permit as specified in Section 17B:17-13.1 of the New Jersey Statutes (Chapter 144, Laws of 1971) and in order that the Insurance Department may be fully advised as to the qualifications of

said corporation or association to exercise such privileges in the State of New Jersey, the following facts are submitted:

1. The _____ an association is a corporation which was duly organized under the laws of the State of _____ on the _____ day of _____ 19___ for the purpose of _____

(Indicate whether a corporation or an association and quote powers from certificate of incorporation or articles of association.)

2. Is the corporation or association conducted without profit and engaged solely in bona fide charitable, religious, missionary, educational, or philanthropic activities? Answer _____.

3. Has the corporation or association (including its predecessor corporation or association) been in active operation for at least ten years prior to the date of this application? Answer _____.

4. Will the annuity rates to be charged on new contracts issued on and after January 1, 1973 be sufficient at all ages, on the basis of the 1971 Individual Annuity Mortality table with interest at 6% (or on the basis of any higher permitted standard adopted by the corporation or association for the calculation of its reserves) to return a residuum to the corporation upon death of the annuitant or survivor annuitants of at least 50% of the original gift or consideration? Answer _____.

5. A complete schedule of the present maximum annuity rates of the corporation or association should be attached to this application.

6. Copies of each present form of agreement, currently issued, with annuitants should be attached to this application.

7. Does the financial report which should be submitted herewith show the admitted assets of the corporation or association which on the date of such report had been segregated as separate and distinct funds for the purpose of annuity benefits and which may not, without exception, be applied towards the payment of other debts or obligations of the corporation or association? Answer _____.

8. Attach hereto a certified copy of that portion of the charter, bylaws or the entire resolution requiring segregation of assets for annuity benefits in accordance with the above statute.

Note: See specimen attached of proposed form of resolution satisfactory to this Department.

9. Are such segregated assets held for the protection of *ALL* such annuitants of the corporation? Answer _____.

10. Do such invested assets meet the requirements for the investment of the reserves of authorized life insurance companies? Answer _____.
If not, list or indicate the invested assets which do not comply, and amounts thereof _____.

11. The following represents a summary of the financial report submitted herewith relating to the segregated funds mentioned in Interrogatory (7) above:

Total Admitted Assets _____ Reserve on Annuities
per Actuary's Report _____

217

Amounts past due and
unpaid to Annuitants _____
Other Liabilities _____
Unassigned Funds
(Surplus) _____

Total _____ Total _____

_____   _____

Dated _____
(Name of corporation or association)
SEAL   By _____President
By _____Treasurer

State of _____
ss:
County of _____

_____ and _____ being duly severally sworn, each for himself
deposes and says that the said _____ is the President and the
said _____ is the Treasurer of the _____ ;
_____ trustees
that he signed the foregoing application by order of the board of directors, that
he has read the application and knows the contents thereof and the statements
contained therein and that such application and the data submitted to the
Actuary as the basis of his certificate of valuation are true and complete to the
best of his knowledge, information and belief.

_____
President

_____
Treasurer

Subscribed and sworn to before me this _____ day of _____ 19_____.

SEAL

Certificate of the Valuation of the
Annuity Liability of the

_____
as of _____

State of _____
ss:
County of _____

_____ Actuary, for the _____

deposes and says:

That the amount of the annuity reserve of $_____ shown in the financial
report herewith submitted has been correctly computed based upon the
scheduled and other valuation data submitted to him; that the bases used in
the valuation are shown below and that such bases satisfy the minimum
requirements of the New Jersey Insurance Laws.

Appendix Two

Annuity Table of Mortality	Assumed Rate of Interest	Years of Issue of Annuity Contracts	Amount of Reserve	Deduct Reinsurance Annuity Reserve	Net Annuity Reserve

Total _____

Actuary _____

Subscribed and sworn to before me this _____ day of _____ 19____.

SEAL

_____
Notary Public

PROPOSED FORM OF RESOLUTION TO BE PASSED BY A QUALIFIED NONPROFIT CORPORATION OR ASSOCIATION RELATING TO AN APPLICATION FOR A SPECIAL PERMIT FOR ANNUITY AGREEMENTS WITH DONORS AND THE SEGREGATION OF ASSETS AS FUNDS RESPECTING ANNUITY AGREEMENTS*

WHEREAS, Chapter 144 of the Laws of 1971 established Subtitle 3, Life and Health Insurance Code to be known as Title 17B, Insurance, of the New Jersey Statutes and Section 17B:17-13.1, effective January 1, 1972, provides, among other things in respect to the exemption from certain provisions of the Insurance Law of the State of New Jersey, that a qualified nonprofit domestic or foreign corporation or association organized without capital stock or not for profit, engaged solely in bona fide charitable, religious, missionary, educational or philanthropic activities and which shall have been in active operation for at least ten years prior to the application for a permit hereinafter mentioned, and which enters into annuity agreements with donors, shall segregate from its assets as separate and distinct funds, independent from all other funds of such corporation or association, an amount at least equal to the sum of the reserves on outstanding annuity agreements plus a minimum surplus as required therein on all gift annuity agreements, and shall not apply said segregated assets for the payment of the debts and obligations of the corporation or association or for any purpose other than the annuity benefits therein specified, and,

WHEREAS, this Section on Charitable Annuities provides for the issuance of a special permit by the Commissioner of Insurance of the State of New Jersey for the purposes therein mentioned,

(continued on page 228)

*This proposed form of resolution would be satisfactory to the New Jersey Insurance department.

219

TABLE 11

State Laws Regulating

State	Registration of Licensing	Regulatory Agency	Cost Limitations
Arkansas	Registration	Secretary of State Little Rock Arkansas 72201 501-374-1628	None
California	Registration	Attorney General 3580 Wilshire Blvd. Los Angeles, CA 90010 213-736-2304	None
Connecticut	Registration	Assistant Attorney General 165 Capitol Hartford, CT 06115 203-566-3035	25% to 50% depending on total raised
District of Columbia	Licensing	Chief Business Licensing Branch Dept. of Economic Development 614 ``H'' St., NW Room 101 Washington, DC 20001 202-727-3645	None
Florida	Registration (Names of all fund-raising employees must be registered)	Department of State Division of Licensing The Capitol Tallahassee, FL 32301 904-488-5381	25% to a professional solicitor
Georgia	Registration	Secretary of State State Capitol Atlanta, GA 30334 404-656-2859	None
Hawaii	Registration	Department of Regulatory Agencies Hawaii State Capitol Honolulu, Hawaii 96813 808-548-4740	10% to professional solicitors
Illinois	Registration	Attorney General State of Illinois 188 West Randolph Room 1826 Chicago, IL 60601 312-793-2595	25% to supplier of unordered goods or less than 75% of gross receipts to charitable purpose
Iowa	Licensing	Secretary of State Des Moines Iowa 50319 515-281-5164	None

Charltable Solicitations

Charitable Organizations			Fund-Raising Counsel	
Annual Financial Reporting Requirements	**Monetary Exemption Ceiling**	**Charitable Solicitation Disclosure**	**Registration or Licensing**	**Bonding Requirement**
By March 31 or within 90 days after close of fiscal year	$1,000	None	Registration	$5,000
End of year	None	"Sale for charitable purpose card" must be shown if merchandise is sold for charity	None	None
In form described by Department within 5 months of close of fiscal year and must be audited by an independent accountant if contributions exceed $25,000	$5,000	None	Registration	$10,000
Within 30 days after the end of a licensing period and 30 days after a demand by the mayor (formerly the commissioner)	$1,500	Solicitors must present solicitation in-formation card to prospective donor. Card is issued by Department of Economic Development	Licensing	None
With annual registration process on forms audited by an independent public accountant if in excess of $25,000	$4,000	Organizations must furnish authorization to solicitors which must be exhibited on request	Licensing (Statute refers only to professional solicitors)	$10,000
Within 90 days after close of fiscal or calendar year	None	None	Registration	$5,000
With registration statement	$4,000	Solicitors must furnish authorization on request	Licensing	$5,000
Within six months after end of fiscal or calendar year	$4,000	None	Registration	$5,000
During month of December	None	None	None	None

State	Registration of Licensing	Regulatory Agency	Cost Limitations
Kansas	Registration	Secretary of State State Capitol Building Topeka, KS 66612 913-296-2215	At least 75% of gross receipts must be used for charitable purposes and not more than 25% for the cost of unordered merchandise
Kentucky	Registration	Bureau of Corrections and Attorney General Frankfort, KY 40601 502-564-6607	15% of gross contributions of money and property received and net proceeds for sales of goods and services
**Maine	Registration	Secretary of State Augusta, ME 04330 207-289-3716	None
Maryland	Registration	Secretary of State State House Annapolis, MD 21414 301-269-3421	25% unless higher is authorized
Massachusetts	Licensing	Attorney General Division of Public Charities Boston, MA 02108 617-727-2235	15% to a professional solicitor; 50% overall solicitation expense; unless higher is proven to be in public interest
Michigan	Licensing	Attorney General Law Building Lansing, MI 48913 517-373-1152	None
Minnesota	Registration	Special Asst. Attorney General 515 Transportation Bldg. St. Paul, MN 55155 612-296-6438	30% for administration, general and fund-raising costs is presumed to be unreasonable
Nebraska	Certificate granted on basis of letter of approval obtained from county attorney of home-office county	Secretary of State Lincoln, NE 68509 402-471-2554	None
Nevada	None	Attorney General Carson City, NE 89701 702-855-4170	None

222

Annual Financial Reporting Requirements	Monetary Exemption Ceiling	Charitable Solicitation Disclosure	Registration or Licensing	Bonding Requirement
Appropriate form pursuant to the Kansas Statutes Annotated Sec. 17-7500 et. seq.	$5,000 (If all Fund Raising is by volunteers)	None	Registration	$5,000
None	None	Registration receipt must be shown to donor	Registration (with county clerk)	None
Within six months after close of fiscal year	$10,000	No professional fund raiser or solicitor shall solicit funds for a charitable purpose without full disclosure to the prospective donor the estimated cost of solicitation where less than 70% of amount donated will be expended for the specific charitable purpose	Registration	$10,000
Most recent completed fiscal year. If in excess of $100,000 an audit is required by an independent certified public accountant according to the standards of accounting and financial reporting of voluntary health and welfare organizations	$5,000	None	Registration	$10,000
On or before June 1 or before 60 days following a fiscal year ending in April or May on prescribed forms	$5,000	Solicitors must exhibit authorization on request	Licensing	$10,000
With application for license or renewal for 12-month period immediately preceding the time it files	$8,000	License or registration number must be written on solicitation materials	Licensing	$10,000
Within six months of the fiscal or calendar year. CPA statement needed if more than $25,000 is raised	$10,000 If only volunteers used	Solicitation card must be shown prior to solicitation	Licensing	up to $20,000
Within 6 months after the close of the calendar or fiscal year	None	Solicitor must carry and show certificate	None	None
By July 1 with Secretary of State	None	None	None	None

State	Registration of Licensing	Regulatory Agency	Cost Limitations
New Hampshire	Licensing	Secretary of State Division of Welfare Concord, NH 03301 603-271-3272	85% must be applied to a charitable purpose
New Jersey	Registration	Attorney General State House Annex Trenton, NJ 08625 609-292-4925	15% to professional fund-raiser and professional solicitor 50% for mail solicitation via unordered merchandise
New York	Registration	Office of Charities Registration Department of State Albany, NY 12231 518-474-3720	50% for mail solicitation via unordered merchandise
North Carolina	Licensing	Department of Human Resources Raleigh, NC 27605 919-733-4510	5% to professional solicitor 35% for solicitation & fund-raising expenses, unless approved for higher (including payments and salaries)
North Dakota	Licensing	Secretary of State Bismarck, ND 58501 701-224-2901	35% re-solicitation of fund-raising expenses (including payment to professional solicitor or fund-raiser) 15% to fund-raisers of solicitors
Ohio	Registration	Attorney General Columbus, OH 43215 614-466-3180	None
Oklahoma	Registration	Commission of Charities and Corrections State Capitol, Rm. 8 Oklahoma City, OK 73105 405-521-3495	Payments to professional fund-raisers or solicitors limited to 10% of totals raised
Oregon	Registration	Attorney General Portland, OR 97201 503-229-5278	25% for solicitation, 50% overall
Pennsylvania	Licensing	Commission on Charitable Organizations Dept. of State Harrisburg, PA 17120 717-783-1720	35% re-solicitation & fund-raising expenses (including payment to professional solicitor and fund-raiser) 15% to professional solicitor
Rhode Island	Registration	Department of Business Regulations Providence, RI 02903 401-277-2405	50% re-solicitation of fund-raising expenses, 25% to professional solicitor
**South Carolina	Registration	Secretary of State Columbia, SC 29211 803-758-2244	Reasonable percentage to professional solicitor
South Dakota	Registration	Department of Commerce and Consumer Protection State Capitol Bldg. Pierre, SD 57501 605-773-3696	30% to professional fund-raiser

Annual Financial Reporting Requirements	Monetary Exemption Ceiling	Charitable Solicitation Disclosure	Registration or Licensing	Bonding Requirement
When requested by the director of the division	None	None	None	None
Within 6 months after close of fiscal or calendar year	$10,000	None	Registration	$10,000
Within 90 days after the close of its fiscal year. If in excess of $50,000 for preceding year, report must be accompanied by an opinion signed by an independent public accountant	$10,000	None	Registration	$5,000
With application for license per "Audit guide" of American Institute of Certified Public Accountants (simplified reporting for organizations raising under $25,000)	$2,000	Solicitor must show authorization on request. Receipt must be issued for contribution over $5	Licensing	$5,000
Within 60 days after the close the fiscal or calendar year if any contributions were received during the previous calendar year	None	None	Registration	None
By March 31 if on a calendar year; if on a fiscal year 90 days of close of fiscal year	None	None	Registration	$5,000
Within 90 days of the end of the fiscal or calendar year	None	Receipts must be given for contributions over $2	Registration	$2,500
Within four months of close of calendar or fiscal year	$250	None	None	None
Submitted with annual licensing process	$7,500	Solicitor must produce authorization on request	Licensing	$10,000
Within 90 days after end of fiscal year audited by an independent certified accountant	$3,000	Solicitor must produce authorization on request	Registration	$10,000
Within six months of the close of the fiscal year	$2,000	Solicitor must produce authorization on request	Registration	$5,000
An independent audited annual report for contributions received of $10,000 or more as prescribed by National Health Council, National Assembly of National Voluntary Health and Social Welfare Organization Standards and forms	$2,000	None	Licensing	$20,000

State	Registration of Licensing	Regulatory Agency	Cost Limitations
Tennessee	Registration	Secretary of State Capitol Hill Bldg. Nashville, TN 37219 615-741-2078	25% for fund-raising costs
**Texas	None	Katherine Chapman Ass't. Atty. Gen. P.O. Box 12548 Austin, TX 78711 512-475-4651	None
Virginia	Registration	Administrator of Consumer Affairs Richmond, VA 23219 804-786-2043	To professional solicitor — 15% of gross amount collected or 10% of amount received from public support
Washington	Licensing	Department of Licensing Olympia, WA 98501 206-753-1966	20% unless higher is approved
West Virginia	Registration	Secretary of State Capitol Bldg. Charleston, WV 25305 304-348-2112	15% to professional solicitor
Wisconsin	Registration	Department of Registration & Licensing Madison, WI 53702 608-266-0829	None

** **Religious Exemption** - religious organizations and affiliates exempt for all states except:

Maine: Exempt except to the extent "that the organization engages in the solicitation of funds or sales of goods or services to the general public by means of advertisements, personal contacts, mailings or telephone."

Minnesota: Exempt under US District Court decision of 1/21/80; State has appealed. Exemption continued until decision received on appeal.

South Carolina: Exempt when solicitation is confined to "members, their families, corporations, foundations or trustees of employees of such organizations."

Texas: Exempt when limited to "churches, ecclesiastical or denominational organizations or other established physical places for worship at which religious services are the primary activity and such activities are regularly conducted."

226

Annual Financial Reporting Requirements	Monetary Exemption Ceiling	Charitable Solicitation Disclosure	Registration or Licensing	Bonding Requirement
Submitted as part of annual registration process	$10,000	None	Registration	$10,000
Books available at charity's premises for three years.	$10,000	None	None	None
Submitted as part of annual registration process	$2,000	Solicitors must produce authorization on request and furnish receipts for contributions of $5 or more	Registration	$5,000
Within 90 days after the close of the fiscal year also at discretion of Dept. within 30 days after close of any special solicitation	$10,000	Solicitors must identify themselves	Registration	$5,000
Financial report must accompany annual registration statement and if in excess of $50,000 required to have an audit by an independent public accountant	$7,500	None	Registration	$10,000
Within 6 months of the close of the fiscal or calendar year	$500	None	Registration	$5,000

*Information in this table appeared in the December 1979 issue of GIVING USA, published by the American Association of Fund-Raising Counsel, Inc. (New York, N.Y.). Used by permission.

Now, therefore, to be RESOLVED that in order to meet the aforementioned requirements of the law and for the purpose of obtaining a special permit from the Commissioner of Insurance of the State of New Jersey to issue gift annuity agreements in New Jersey there shall be set aside and maintained assets of the corporation or association as separate and distinct funds independent of all other funds of the corporation or association in an amount which is at least equal to the sum of reserves and of surplus as required by this Section and which shall be invested as provided in this Section and that such segregated funds shall not be applied for the payment of the debts and obligations of the corporation or association or for any purpose other than the annuity benefits herein referred to and which fund shall be known as _____
_____ (use a name that will clearly designate it as the segregated assets account contemplated by this Section.)

Any assets heretofore segregated and held as separate funds on account of annuity benefits shall be merged with the aforesaid segregated assets to the extent required in order to comply with the provisions of Section 17B:17-13.1 of the New Jersey Statutes.

In addition to specific state legislation regulating gift annuities, an organization should also be aware of the fact that some blue sky laws in various states may consider the gift annuity to be a security. In those cases, the charitable organization should be sure that it is either exempt under the statutes or receives a no-action letter before issuing annuities in those states. This same application can be made to pooled income funds, which most states consider securities but will grant an exemption for. In conclusion, be sure to check with legal counsel before making an offering on any type of charitable gift which offers a life income return.

Appendix Three
SAMPLE

Charitable Remainder Annuity Trust—Two Lives

NOTE: This legal instrument is a SAMPLE only. State laws vary widely; therefore, this document should not be used without first consulting your own legal counsel. The use of generalized documents for specific applications is not recommended.

This CHARITABLE REMAINDER ANNUITY TRUST AGREEMENT is made and entered into this _____ day of _____, 19___, between _____ of _____ County of _____, State of _____, (hereinafter called the "Donor"), and _____, a corporation duly existing under the laws of the State of _____ and located in _____ in said State (hereinafter called the Trustee).

Article I

The Trustee acknowledges receipt of the property listed on Exhibit A attached hereto as an irrevocable gift from the Donor, which property shall be held and administered IN TRUST as follows.

Article II

This Annuity Trust shall be designated on the books and records of the Trustee as the _____ Fund.

Article III

Neither the Donor nor any other person may at any time make additional contributions to the annuity trust.

Article IV

The Trustee is authorized to continue investment of the trust in the assets set forth in Exhibit A or may sell said assets and reinvest the trust assets in any manner consistent with Section 664 of the Internal Revenue Code and the Regulations thereunder. Nothing in this trust instrument shall be construed to restrict the Trustee from investing the trust assets in a manner which could result in the annual realization of a reasonable amount of income or gain from sale or disposition of trust assets.

Article V

During the lifetime of the Donor, the Trustee shall annually pay the Donor _____ dollars or ____ percent of the initial net fair market value of all property placed in trust, whichever is greater. This amount shall be paid from income, and, to the extent that income is insufficient, from principal. Any income of the trust for the taxable year in excess of the amount required to be paid under this paragraph shall be added to principal. If the Donor's wife, _____ (hereinafter referred to as "Donor's wife"), survives the Donor, this amount shall be paid to her during her lifetime. However, the Donor hereby reserves the right to appoint and direct by his will, but only by express reference to this agreement, that all of the trust assets shall be irrevocably transferred to the Trustee upon his death subject to the provisions of Article X, whether or not the Donor's wife survives the Donor. Except in the case of a short taxable year, the amount required to be distributed above shall be paid during every taxable year of the trust. This amount shall be paid in four quarterly payments on or after March 31, June 30, September 30, and December 31 of each taxable year of the trust. However, the obligation of the Trustee to make payments to the Donor hereunder shall terminate with the regular quarterly payment next preceding the death of the Donor. If the Donor's wife survives the Donor and the Donor has failed to exercise the above-mentioned power of appointment, then the obligation of the Trustee to make payments to the Donor's wife hereunder shall begin with the next regular quarterly payment after the Donor's death and shall terminate with the regular quarterly payment next preceding the Donor's wife's death.

Article VI

In determining the annuity amount, the Trustee shall prorate the same on a daily basis for a short taxable year and the taxable year of the death of the last surviving income beneficiary hereunder.

Article VII

The taxable year of this trust shall be the year ending December 31.

Article VIII

In the case where the initial net fair market value of the trust assets is incorrectly determined, the Trustee shall pay to the income beneficiary in the case of undervaluation, or the income beneficiary shall repay to the Trustee in the case of an overvaluation, an amount equal to the difference between the amount which the trust should have paid if the correct value were used and the amount which the trust actually paid, within a reasonable period after the final determination of such value.

Article IX

For the purposes of this trust, the term "income" has the same meaning as it does under Section 643(B) of the Internal Revenue Code and the Regulations thereunder. The term "income" shall mean net income after payment of any reasonable expenses of administering the trust. The following shall be treated as principal and not as "income":
  (a) Gains and losses from the sale, exchange, redemption, or other disposition of investments;
  (b) Stock dividends, stock splits, or similar distributions;

(c) Capital gain dividends of regulated investment companies (mutual funds);

(d) Liquidating distributions.

Article X

Upon the death of the survivor of the Donor and the Donor's wife (or upon the death of the Donor if the Donor exercises the power of appointment under Article 5), the trust assets shall be irrevocably transferred to the "ABC" charitable institution to be used in such manner as the trustees thereof may direct.

Article XI

In the event the "ABC" charitable institution is not an organization described in sections 170(c), 2055(a) and 2522(a) or (b) of the Internal Revenue Code at the time when any amount is to be irrevocably transferred to the said institution, such amount shall be transferred to or for the use of an organization or organizations, selected by the Trustee in its sole discretion, which are described in the said Sections, or retained for such use.

Article XII

It is the intention of the Donor and the Trustee in executing this agreement to create a Charitable Remainder Annuity Trust within the meaning of Section 664 of the Internal Revenue Code and the Regulations thereunder. All the provisions hereof shall be interpreted in a manner consistent with the regulations and rulings promulgated by the Internal Revenue Service with respect thereto. Otherwise, this instrument shall be governed by the laws of the State of _____.

Article XIII

Anything herein to the contrary notwithstanding, the assets of the trust estate shall not be subject to claim for any Federal, state or other estate, inheritance or succession taxes or duties which may be assessed against the estate of the Donor or against any beneficiary hereunder, and the Donor agrees to make no inconsistent provision in his Will.

Article XIV

Notwithstanding any other provision hereof, payments for each taxable year shall be made at such time and in such manner as not to subject the trust to tax under IRC §4942. Except for the payment of the annuity amount to the beneficiary, the Trustee shall not engage in any act of self-dealing (as defined in §4941(d) of the Internal Revenue Code of 1954, as amended); nor shall the Trustee make any taxable expenditures (as defined in §4945(d) of the said Code); nor shall the Trustee make any investments which jeopardize the charitable purpose of the Annuity Trust (as defined in §4944 of said Code; or retain any excess business holdings (within the meaning of §4943 of the said Code).

Article XV

(a) Except as provided in this paragraph, this instrument may be amended, altered or modified at any time or from time to time, in writing, by the Trustee.

(b) In the event that an amendment affects the rights or obligations of any income beneficiary hereunder, such amendment shall not become effective until the first day of the calendar month following sixty days after a copy of such amendment shall have been mailed to each such beneficiary. If such income beneficiary shall file with the Trustee a notice in writing objecting to such amendment, and if such notice is received by the Trustee at least five days prior to the effective date of the amendment, such amendment shall be void.

(c) Notwithstanding any other provision of this paragraph, no amendment shall be made which affects the irrevocable remainder interest granted to the Trustee in all property held in the trust, or which otherwise affects the qualification of the trust as a charitable remainder annuity trust within the meaning of §664 of the Internal Revenue Code, as that term is defined from time to time in said Code, and the Trustee shall have the power to amend this instrument for the purpose of preserving such qualification without reference to the limitations set forth in subparagraph (b) of this paragraph.

Article XVI

The Trustee shall have all the powers conferred upon trustees by the Uniform Trustees' Powers Act except to the extent limited by this agreement and Section 664 of the Internal Revenue Code.

Article XVII

The Trustee shall not receive any compensation for services rendered under this agreement, excepting a reasonable investment management fee. No bond shall be required of the Trustee.

Article XVIII

This agreement shall be effective only upon execution by the Trustee at its offices at _____.

IN WITNESS WHEREOF, the parties have set their hands and seals hereto in duplicate the day, month, and year herein above first written.

In the presence of

_____   _____

                               Donor

_____ By _____ (SEAL)

                               Name:

                               Title:

Appendix Four
SAMPLE

Charitable Remainder Unitrust Agreement—Two Lives

NOTE: This legal instrument is a SAMPLE only. State laws vary widely; therefore, this document should not be used without first consulting your own legal counsel. The use of generalized documents for specific applications is not recommended.

This CHARITABLE REMAINDER UNITRUST AGREEMENT is made and entered into this _____ day of _____, 19___, between _____ of _____ County of _____, State of _____ (hereinafter called the "Donor") and _____ a corporation duly existing under the laws of the State of _____, and located in _____ in said State (hereinafter called the Trustee).

Article I

The trustee acknowledged receipt of the property listed on Exhibit A attached hereto as an irrevocable gift from the Donor, which property and all additions thereto shall be held and administered in trust as follows.

Article II

This Unitrust shall be designated on the books and records of the Trustee as the _____Fund.

Article III

The Donor or any other person may at any time make additional contributions to this Unitrust by gift or bequest with the consent of the Trustee.

Article IV

The Trustee is authorized to continue investment of the trust in the assets set forth in Exhibit A or may sell said assets and reinvest the trust assets in any manner consistent with Section 664 of the Internal Revenue Code and the Regulations thereunder. Nothing in this trust instrument shall be construed to restrict the Trustee from investing the trust assets in a manner which could result in the annual realization of a reasonable amount of income or gain from the sale or disposition of trust assets.

Article V

ALTERNATIVE A. During the lifetime of the Donor, the Trustee shall pay the Donor in each taxable year an amount equal to ＿＿ percent (must be at least 5 percent) of the net fair market value of the assets of the trust determined annually in accordance with ARTICLE IX. This amount shall be paid from income or, to the extent that income is insufficient, from principal. Any income of the trust for the taxable year in excess of the amount required to be paid under this paragraph shall be added to principal.

ALTERNATIVE B. During the lifetime of the Donor, the Trustee shall pay the Donor the amount of the trust income to the extent that such amount does not exceed ＿＿ percent (must be at least 5 percent) of the net fair market value of the trust assets determined annually in accordance with ARTICLE IX. Any income of the trust for the taxable year in excess of the amount required to be paid under this paragraph shall be added to principal.

ALTERNATIVE C. During the lifetime of the Donor, the Trustee shall pay the Donor the amount of the trust income to the extent that such amount does not exceed ____ percent (must be at least five percent) of the net fair market value of the trust assets determined annually in accordance with ARTICLE IX. If the trust income in any taxable year exceeds ____ percent of the net fair market value of assets determined annually, such excess income shall be distributed to the Donor to the extent that the aggregate of the percentage amount paid in prior years was less than the aggregate amounts required to be paid hereunder. Any income of the trust for the taxable year in excess of the amount required to be paid under this paragraph shall be added to principal.

If the Donor's wife _____ (hereinafter referred to as "Donor's wife") survives the Donor, the Trustee shall pay this amount to her during her lifetime. However, the Donor hereby reserves the right to appoint and direct by his Will, but only by express reference to this agreement, that all of the trust assets shall be irrevocably transferred to the Trustee upon his death, subject to the provisions of ARTICLE XIII hereafter, whether or not the Donor's wife survives the Donor. The Trustee may rely on any instrument admitted to probate in any jurisdiction as the Will of the Donor, or, if the Trustee has no notice or knowledge of the existence of such Will within four months after the Donor's death, it may act upon the assumption that he died intestate.

Except in the case of a short taxable year, the amount required to be distributed above shall be paid during every taxable year of the trust.

This amount shall be paid in four quarterly payments on or after March 31, June 30, September 30, and December 31. However, the obligation of the Trustee to make payments to the Donor hereunder shall terminate with the regular quarterly payment next preceding the death of the Donor. If the Donor's wife survives the Donor and the Donor has failed to exercise the above-mentioned power of appointment, then the obligation of the Trustee to make payments to the Donor's wife hereunder shall begin with the next quarterly payment after the Donor's death and shall terminate with the regular quarterly payment next preceding the Donor's wife's death.

Article VI

In determining the unitrust amount the Trustee shall prorate the same on a daily basis for a short taxable year and the taxable year of the death of the last surviving income beneficiary hereunder.

Article VII

If any additional contributions are made to the trust after the initial contribution in trust, the unitrust amount for the taxable year in which the assets are added shall be ____ percent (same percentage as ARTICLE V) of the sum of (a) the net fair market of trust assets (excluding the added assets and any income from, or appreciation on, such assets) and (b) that proportion of the value of the added assets that was excluded under (a) which the number of days in the period beginning with the date of contribution and ending with the earlier of the last day of the taxable year or the date of the expiration of all noncharitable interests hereunder bears to the number of days in the period beginning with the first day of such taxable year and ending with the earlier of the last day in such taxable year or the date of the expiration of noncharitable interests. In the case where there is no valuation date after the time of contribution, the assets so added shall be valued at the time of contribution.

An additional contribution made by way of bequest, devise, or transfer from a trust by reason of death shall be deemed to have been made on the date of the decedent's death even though the distribution is not made until the end of a reasonable period for administration or settlement of the estate or trust. The Trustee shall be required to pay the beneficiary or beneficiaries hereunder the amount provided in ARTICLE V with respect to such additional contribution beginning as of the date of death of the decedent even though the requirement to pay such amount is deferred until the additional contribution is actually received. Within a reasonable period after the receipt in full of the additional contribution, the Trustee shall pay (in the case of underpayment) or there shall be received from the recipient (in the case of overpayment) the difference between the total of any unitrust amounts actually paid and the total of such amounts payable plus interest at 6 percent compounded annually. The amount which is payable shall be retroactively determined by using the taxable year, valuation method and dates which have been adopted by the trust and shall be computed in accordance with Regulation S 1.664-1 (a) (5) (ii).

Article VIII

The taxable year of this trust shall be the year ending December 31.

Article IX

The trust assets, including additional contributions, shall be valued on the last business day of the first month of the taxable year. Except for the valuation of added contributions as provided for in ARTICLE VII above, if no valuation date occurs before the end of any taxable year of the trust, the assets shall be valued on the last day of the taxable year of the trust, or as of the date on which all noncharitable interests terminate.

Article X

In computing the net fair market value of the assets, all accrued assets and accrued liabilities will be taken into account.

Article XI

In the case where the net fair market value of the trust assets is incorrectly determined, the Trustee shall pay to the income beneficiary in the case of an undervaluation, or the income beneficiary shall repay to the Trustee in the case of an overvaluation, an amount equal to the difference between the amount which the trust should have paid, if the correct value were used and the amount which the trust actually paid, within a reasonable period after the final determination of such value.

Article XII

For the purposes of this trust, the term "income" has the same meaning as it does under Section 643 (b) of the Internal Revenue

Code and Regulations thereunder. The term "income" shall mean net income after payment of any reasonable expenses of administering the trust. The following shall be treated as principal and not as "income":
  (a) Gains and losses from the sale, exchange, redemption, or other disposition of investments;
  (b) Stock dividends, stock splits, or similar distributions;
  (c) Capital gain dividends of regulated investment companies (mutual funds);
  (d) Liquidating distributions.

Article XIII

Upon the death of the survivor of the Donor and the Donor's wife (or upon the death of the Donor if the Donor exercises the power of appointment under ARTICLE V, the trust assets shall be irrevocably transferred to XYZ Charitable Organization.

Article XIV

In the event the "XYZ" charitable institution is not an organization described in Section 170 (c) and 2055 (a) or 2522 (a) or (b) of the Internal Revenue Code at the time when any amount is to be irrevocably transferred to said institution, such amount shall be transferred to or for the use of an organization or organizations selected by the Trustee in its sole discretion which are described in the said Section, or retained for such use.

Article XV

It is the intention of the Donor and the Trustee in executing this agreement to create a Charitable Remainder Unitrust within the meaning of Section 664 of the Internal Revenue Code and the Regulations thereunder. All the provisions hereof shall be interpreted in a manner consistent with the Regulations and Rulings promulgated by the Internal Revenue Service with respect thereto. Otherwise, this instrument shall be governed by the laws of the State of _____.

Article XVI

Anything herein to the contrary notwithstanding, the assets of the trust estate shall not be subject to claim for any federal, state or other estate, inheritance or succession taxes or duties which may be assessed against the estate of the Donor or against any beneficiary hereunder, and the Donor agrees to make no inconsistent provision in his will.

Article XVII

Notwithstanding any other provision hereof, the unitrust amount for each taxable year shall be distributed at such time and in such manner as not to subject the trust to tax under IRS §4942, except for the payment of the unitrust amount to the beneficiary. The Trustee shall not engage in any act of self-dealing (as defined in §4941 (d) of said Code). The Trustee shall not make any investments which jeopardize the charitable purpose of the unitrust (as defined in §4944 (d) of the Internal Revenue Code of 1954 as amended); nor make any taxable expenditures (as defined in §4945(d) of said Code). The Trustee shall not make any investments which jeopardize the charitable purpose of the unitrust (as defined in §4945 (d) of said Code, nor retain any excess business holdings (within the meaning of §4943 of the said Code).

Article XVIII

(a) Except as provided in this paragraph, this instrument may be amended, altered or modified at any time or from time to time, in writing, by the Trustee.

(b) In the event that an amendment affects the rights or obligations of any income beneficiary hereunder, such amendment shall not become effective until the first day of the calendar month following sixty days after a copy of such amendment shall have been mailed to each such beneficiary. If such income beneficiary shall file with the Trustee a notice in writing objecting to such amendment, and if such notice is received by the Trustee at least five days prior to the effective date of the amendment, such amendment shall be void.

(c) Notwithstanding any other provision of this paragraph, no amendment shall be made which affects the irrevocable remainder interest granted to the Trustee in all property held in the trust, or which otherwise affects the qualification of the trust as a charitable remainder unitrust within the meaning of §664 of the Internal Revenue Code, as that term is defined from time to time in said Code, and the Trustee shall have the power to amend this instrument for the purposes of preserving such qualification without reference to the limitations set forth in subparagraph (b) of this paragraph.

Article XIX

The trustee shall have all the powers conferred upon trustees by the Uniform Trustees' Powers Act except to the extent limited by this agreement and Section 664 of the Internal Revenue Code.

Article XX

The trustee shall not receive any compensation for services rendered under this agreement, excepting a reasonable investment management fee. No bond shall be required of the Trustee.

Article XXI

This agreement shall be effective only upon execution by the Trustee at its offices at _____.

IN WITNESS WHEREOF, the parties have set their hands and seals hereto in duplicate the day, month, and year hereinabove first written.

In the presence of

_____   _____(SEAL)
                               DONOR

_____   _____(SEAL)
                               TRUSTEE
                               Name:
                               Title:

Appendix Five
SAMPLE

Declaration of Trust
Pooled Income Fund

NOTE: This legal instrument is a SAMPLE only. State laws vary widely; therefore, this document should not be used without first consulting your own legal counsel. The use of generalized documents for specific applications is not recommended.

The _____, a _____
_____, of _____, _____ (hereinafter referred to as Trustee), by executing this master agreement on this _____ day of _____, 19___, hereby establishes the (name of institution or organization) _____
Pooled Income Fund (hereinafter referred to as the "Fund") as defined in Section 642(c)(5) of the Internal Revenue Code of 1954 as amended.

Article I

Each donor transferring property to the Fund shall contribute an irrevocable remainder interest in such property to the Trustee.

Article II

Each donor transferring property to the Fund shall retain for himself an income interest in the property transferred, or create an income interest in such property for life of one or more named beneficiaries, each of whom must be living at the time of the transfer of the property to the Fund by the donor. In the event more than one beneficiary of the income interest is named, such beneficiaries may enjoy their shares of income concurrently and/or consecutively. The donor need not retain or create a life interest in all the income from the property transferred to the Fund provided any income not payable to an income beneficiary is contributed to and within the taxable year in which it is received, to a qualified charitable organization.

Article III

The property transferred to the Fund by each donor must be commingled with, and invested or reinvested with, other property transferred to the Fund by other donors satisfying the requirements of this instrument and of provisions of the Internal Revenue Code of 1954, as now and hereafter amended, governing Pooled Income Funds. The Fund shall not include property transferred under arrangements other than those specified in this instrument and satisfying the said provisions of the Internal Revenue Code. All or any portion of the Fund may, however, be invested or reinvested jointly with other properties, not a part of this Fund, which are held by the Trustee in a common trust fund to which Internal Revenue Code Section 584 applies for the collective investment and reinvestment of monies of such funds. When such joint investment or reinvestment occurs, detailed accounting records shall be maintained specifically identifying the portions of the Fund and the income earned by, and attributable to, such portions.

Article IV

The property transferred to the Fund by any donor shall not include any securities, the income from which is exempt from tax under Subtitle A of the Internal Revenue Code of 1954, and the Trustee shall not accept or invest in any such security as part of the Fund.

Article V

The charitable organization shall always maintain control, directly or indirectly, over the Fund. The charitable organization may designate a new trustee or trustees so long as it retains the power to remove the trustee or trustees and to designate a new trustee or trustees.

Article VI

The Fund shall not have as trustee a donor to the Fund or a beneficiary of an income interest in any property transferred to the Fund. No donor or beneficiary shall have, directly or indirectly, general responsibilities with respect to the Fund which are ordinarily exercised by a trustee.

Article VII

The taxable year of the Fund shall be the calendar year. The Trustee shall pay to each beneficiary entitled to income of any taxable year of the Fund, such income in the amount determined by the rate of return earned by the Fund for such taxable year with respect to his income interest, computed as provided below, at least once in the taxable year in which the income is earned. Until the Trustee determines that payments shall be made more or less frequently or at other times, the Trustee shall make income payments to the beneficiary or beneficiaries entitled thereto in four quarterly payments on or about March 31, June 30, September 30, and December 31 of the taxable year of the Fund. An adjusting payment, if necessary, will be made during the taxable year or within the first sixty-five days following its close to bring the total payment to the actual income to which the beneficiary or beneficiaries were entitled for that year.

Article VIII

Upon the termination of the income interest of the designated beneficiary or beneficiaries, the Trustee shall sever from the Fund an amount equal to the value of the property upon which the income interest is based. The value of the property for such purposes shall be the value as of the date on which the last regular payment was made before the death of the beneficiary as provided in Article IX hereof. The amount so severed from the Fund must either be paid to or retained for the use of a qualified charitable organization for the uses and purposes designated by the donor in the instrument whereby his gift is made, except that in the event _____ is not then an organization described in clauses (i) through (vi) of Section 170(b)(1)(A) of the said Code, such an amount shall be transferred to or for the use of an organization or organizations which are described in the said clauses (i) through (vi) of Section 170(b)(1)(A) of the said Code, provided such organization is also an entity described in Section 2055(a) or 2522(a) or (b) of said Code. The value of the remainder interest for such purposes shall be its value as of the last determination date (as set out in Article X) next succeeding the date of the date of determination of the income interest.

The Trustee shall not be obligated to prorate periodic payments between the estate of a deceased beneficiary and a surviving beneficiary or beneficiaries. The income interest of any beneficiary shall terminate with the regular periodic payment next preceding the date of such beneficiary's death.

Article IX

Every income interest retained or created in property transferred to the Fund shall be assigned a proportionate share of the annual income earned by the Fund, such share or units of participation being based on the fair market value of such property on the date of transfer as provided in this Article. On each transfer of property by a donor to the Fund, there shall be assigned to the beneficiary or beneficiaries of the income interest the number of units of participation equal to the number obtained by dividing the fair market value of the property transferred by the fair market value of a unit in the Fund immediately before such transfer. The fair market value of a unit in the Fund immediately before the transfer shall be determined by dividing the fair market value of all property in the Fund at such time by the number of units then in the Fund. All units in the Fund shall always have equal value. The amount of income allocated to each unit of participation shall be determined by dividing the income of the Fund for the taxable year by the outstanding number of units in the Fund at the end of the year, except that income shall be allocated to units outstanding during only part of such year by taking into consideration the period of time such units are outstanding during such taxable year.

Article X

If possible, each transfer of property by a donor to the Fund and each withdrawal from the Fund as a result of the transfer of the remainder interest in any property of the Fund shall be made only on a determination date of the fair market value of all property held by the Fund. The property of the fund shall be valued on the first day of the taxable year of the Fund and on at least three other days within the taxable year. In no case shall the period between any two consecutive determination dates within the taxable year be greater than three calendar months. If a transfer of property to the fund by a donor occurs on other than a determination date, the number of units of participation assigned to the income interest of such property shall be determined by using the fair market value of the property in the Fund on the determination date immediately preceding the date of transfer (determined without regard to the property so transferred), subject, however, to appropriate adjustments on the next succeeding determination date. In order to make such adjustment, the average fair market value of the property in the fund at the time of the transfer shall be deemed to be the average of the fair market values of the property in the Fund on the determination dates immediately preceding and succeeding the date of transfer. For the purpose of determining such average, any property transferred to the Fund between such preceding and succeeding dates, or on such succeeding date, shall be excluded.

Article XI

Notwithstanding any other provision hereof, the income of the Fund for each taxable year shall be distributed at such time and in such manner as not to subject the trust to tax under Section 4942 of the Internal Revenue Code of 1954 as amended. The Trustee shall not engage in any act of self-dealing (as defined in Section 4941(d) of the said Code); nor shall the Trustee make any taxable expenditures (as defined in Section 4945(d) of the said Code); nor shall the Trustee make any investments which jeopardize the charitable purpose of any gift to the Fund (as defined in Section 4944 of the said Code) or retain any excess business holdings (within the meaning of Section 4943 of the said Code).

Article XII

For the purposes of this trust, the term "income" has the same meaning as it does under Section 643(b) of the Internal Revenue Code and the regulations thereunder. The term "income" shall mean net income after payment of any expenses of administering the trust. Such expenses shall include reasonable investment management, custodial, and like fees. The following shall be treated as principal and not as "income":

(a) Gains and losses from the sale, exchange, redemption, or other disposition of investments;

(b) Stock dividends, stock splits, or similar distributions;

(c) Capital gain dividends of regulated investment companies (mutual funds);

(d) Any other dividends or distributions not deemed taxable as ordinary income under the Internal Revenue Code.

If interest bearing securities are acquired at a premium over par or other stated value, the premium shall be amortized from income so as to restore the premium to principal.

Article XIII

Subject to the provisions of Article IV, the Trustee shall have, in addition to any powers conferred upon it by law, the following powers and discretions:

(a) To retain any property transferred to a donor and to invest and reinvest in and retain all kinds of property of any character, foreign or domestic, real or personal, without being confined to "legal investments."

(b) To sell, exchange or lease for any period of time any property, real or personal; to maintain, repair, alter, improve, restrict, subdivide, develop, partition, dedicate or abandon real estate; to grant easements concerning and to otherwise encumber real estate; and to give options and execute option agreements for the sale or lease of assets held, without obligation to repudiate the same in favor of better offers.

(c) To subscribe for stocks, bonds, or other investments; to join in any plan of lease, mortgage, merger, consolidation, reorganization, foreclosure or voting trust and deposit securities thereunder; to exercise options to purchase stock and other property; and generally to exercise all the rights of security holders of any corporation.

(d) To register securities in street name or in the name of a nominee or in such manner that title shall pass by delivery and to vote, in person or by proxy, securities held hereunder and in such connection to delegate discretionary powers.

(e) To make all reasonable compromises.

(f) To employ and compensate from income or principal, in Trustee's discretion, investment counsel, accountants, brokers, and other specialists, and a corporate custodian.

Article XIV

The principal and the income of the Fund, so long as the same are held by the Trustee, shall be free from the control, debts, liabilities and assignments of any beneficiary interested therein, and shall not be subject to execution or process for the enforcement of judgments or claims of any sort against such beneficiary.

Article XV

This instrument may be and is intended to be incorporated by reference in any will, trust, or other instrument whereby

property is transferred to _____
and an income interest is retained or created for the life of one or more named beneficiaries, each of whom is living at the time of transfer. This instrument, together with any such instrument of transfer, shall together be considered the "governing instrument" for such transfer. Any property transferred to a qualified charitable organization by will or otherwise whereby an income interest is retained or created for the life of one or more named beneficiaries, each of whom is living at the time of transfer, where this instrument is not incorporated by reference, shall be made a part of the Fund and be held, managed, and distributed under the terms of this instrument unless the will or other instrument of transfer is inconsistent with such action by the Trustee.

Article XVI

The purpose of the Fund is to create financial reserves for _____ while, at the same time, affording reasonable returns to individual beneficiaries. It is not the purpose of the Fund to compete with regulated investment companies, commercial annuities, or other forms of investment available to the general public. Solicitation of gifts to the Fund shall not be made from the general public, but only from donors and friends of _____. In order to serve the purpose of the Fund, the trustee shall establish and maintain policies from time to time setting forth minimum ages, maximum number of lives of individual income beneficiaries and the minimum donated amounts of participation in the Fund. The Trustee shall give prior approval to each gift to the Fund before it is made a part of the Fund.

Article XVII

By executing this instrument, _____
intends to qualify the Fund as a Pooled Income Fund within the meaning of Section 642(c)(5) of the Internal Revenue Code of 1954, as amended, and the regulations thereunder. The provisions hereof should be interpreted in accordance with the regulations and rulings promulgated by the Internal Revenue Service with respect to such Funds and contributions to them.

Otherwise, this instrument shall be governed by the laws of the State of _____.

Article XVIII

The power to amend this Pooled Income Fund shall be subject to the following provisions:

(a) Except as provided in this Section, this Declaration of Trust may be amended, altered or modified at any time or from time to time in writing by the Trustee.

(b) In the event that an amendment affects the rights or obligations of any income beneficiary hereunder, such amendment shall not become effective until the first day of the calendar month following sixty days after a copy of such amendment shall have been mailed to each such beneficiary. If such income beneficiary shall file with the trustee a notice in writing objecting to such amendment, and if such notice is received by the trustee at least five days prior to the effective date of the amendment, such amendment shall be void.

(c) Notwithstanding any other provision of this Section, no amendment shall be made which affects the irrevocable remainder interest granted to _____ _____ in all property held in the Fund, or which otherwise affects the qualification of the Fund as a "Pooled Income Fund" within the meaning of Section 642 of the Internal Revenue Code, and the Trustee shall have the power to amend this Declaration of Trust for the purpose of preserving such qualification without reference to the limitations set forth in subparagraph (b) of this Section.

Executed as a sealed instrument this _____ day of _____, 19____.

QUALIFIED CHARITABLE ORGANIZATION

By _____(SEAL)

Name:

Witness: _____ Title:

251

Appendix Six
SAMPLE

Revocable Living Trust Agreement

NOTE: This legal instrument is a SAMPLE only. State laws vary widely; therefore, this document should not be used without first consulting your own legal counsel. The use of generalized documents for specific applications is not recommended.

This Trust Agreement made this 1st day of _____, 19___, by and between _____, _____, hereinafter called the Grantor, and _____, a not-for-profit corporation of _____, _____, hereinafter called the Trustee.

Witnesseth:

That the Grantor has this day delivered to the Trustee the property described in Schedule A attached hereto, and the Trustee agrees to hold, administer and distribute all of the aforesaid assets (together with all additions thereto and all reinvestments thereof) in accordance with the terms and provisions hereinafter set out.

Article I

During the lifetime of the Grantor, the Trustee shall receive, hold and manage the trust property, invest and reinvest said property, collect the income, if any, and shall pay over to or for the benefit of the Grantor during lifetime all of the net income of the trust. The payments shall be made on a quarterly basis on or about June 30, September 30, December 31, and March 31 of each calendar year.

Article II

The Grantor expressly reserves the right, at any time and from time to time during lifetime by a notice in writing filed with the Trustee at least thirty (30) days prior to the effective date thereof, subject to the prior payment of the Trustee's commissions and expenses in respect thereof:

1. To withdraw all or any part of the principal free and discharged of the terms and conditions of this Agreement and of the trust hereby created; and
2. To revoke or amend this Agreement, and to alter or terminate the trust hereby created, provided, however, that the duties and responsibilities of the Trustee as herein provided, shall not be altered or modified by such amendment except upon the written consent of the Trustee.

Article III

Unless sooner terminated, as herein provided, upon the death of the Grantor, this Trust shall terminate and the assets shall be distributed as follows:

1. One hundred per cent (100%) of the trust assets shall go to the _____, a not-for-profit corporation of _____, _____, to be used according to the wishes of their governing Board.

Article IV

The Trustee may resign at any time by giving thirty (30) days written notice to the Grantor. In such event, the Grantor shall have the right to appoint a Successor Trustee and if the Grantor shall so fail to appoint within the thirty (30) day period a Successor Trustee, the Trustee shall have the right to petition a court of competent jurisdiction to appoint a Successor Trustee hereunder. Promptly after receiving notice of the appointment of a Successor Trustee, the Trustee hereunder shall render its final accounting and shall transfer and deliver to such Successor, all trust assets then held by it whereupon it shall have no further duties hereunder; provided, however, that nothing herein shall prevent any Trustee at any time from filing a judicial settlement and accounting with a court of competent jurisdiction. Every Successor Trustee appointed hereunder shall possess and exercise all powers and authority herein conferred upon the original Trustee.

Article V

The Trustee shall have all of the powers contained in the Uniform Trustees' Powers Act as incorporated in the _____ Code Annotated.

Article VI

The Trustee shall be entitled to reasonable compensation for the faithful performance of its duties.

Article VII

The Grantor shall have the right to make additions to this Trust Agreement subject to the consent of the Trustee.

Article VIII

This Agreement shall be construed and regulated in all respects by the laws of the State of _____.

Article IX

The Trustee hereby accepts the Trust herein created.

IN WITNESS WHEREOF: the parties hereto have executed this instrument in duplicate the day and year first above written.

_____ , Grantor

XYZ ORGANIZATION, INC., Trustee

BY _____

_____

(title)

Witnesses:

_____ residing at _____

_____ residing at _____

_____ residing at _____

Appendix Seven
SAMPLE

Warranty Deed

NOTE: This legal instrument is a SAMPLE only. State laws vary widely; therefore, this document should not be used without first consulting your own legal counsel. The use of generalized documents for specific applications is not recommended.

Reference _____

THIS INDENTURE, made and entered into this ____ day of _____, 19____ by and between _____ party of the first part, and _____ party of the second part,

WITNESSETH: That for and in consideration of Ten Dollars ($10.00), cash in hand paid, and other good and valuable considerations, the receipt of all of which is hereby acknowledged, the said party of the first part has bargained and sold and does hereby bargain, sell, convey and confirm unto the said party of the second part the following described real estate, situated and being in _____ County of _____, State of

_____.

TO HAVE AND TO HOLD the aforesaid real estate together with all the appurtenances and hereditaments thereunto belonging or in any wise appertaining unto the said party of the second part, his heirs, successors and assigns in fee simple forever.

The said party of the first part does hereby covenant with the said party of the second part that he is lawfully seized in fee of the aforedescribed real estate; that he has good right to sell and convey the same; that the same is unencumbered, _____

_____

and that the title and quiet possession thereto he will warrant and forever defend against the lawful claims of all persons.

The word "party" as used herein shall mean "parties" if more than one person or entity be referred to, and pronouns shall be construed according to their proper gender and number according to the context hereof.

WITNESS the signature of the party of the first part the day and year first above written.

_____

_____

_____

STATE OF _____, COUNTY OF_____

Before me a Notary Public in and for said State and County, duly commissioned and qualified, personally appeared

_____

to me known to be the person . . . . . described in and who executed the foregoing instrument, and acknowledged that . . . he . . . executed the same for the purposes therein contained.

WITNESS my hand and Notarial Seal at office this ___ day of ___ 19___.

My commission expires _____

_____

Notary Public

Appendix Eight
SAMPLE

Life Estate Agreement

NOTE: This legal instrument is a SAMPLE only. State laws vary widely; therefore, this document should not be used without first consulting your own legal counsel. The use of generalized documents for specific applications is not recommended.

This AGREEMENT made and entered into by and between ___(name)___, of _(city and state)_, hereinafter referred to as Grantor, and _(institution)_, a nonprofit charitable corporation of the State of _____ hereinafter referred to as _____.
WITNESSETH:

WHEREAS Grantor has executed and delivered to _(institution)_ a Warranty Deed conveying to _(institution)_ the following described real estate, to-wit:

(Include property description here)

in which deed Grantor has reserved unto himself a life estate;

IT IS THEREFORE AGREED by and between the parties hereto:

1) That Grantor during the full term of his/her natural life shall be entitled to the right of possession and occupancy in and to the above described real estate and the rents, income and profits arising therefrom.

258

2) That Grantor shall pay the real estate taxes levied and assessed against said real estate during his/her lifetime.

3) That __(institution)__ will not sell or convey its remainder interest in said real estate during the lifetime of Grantor.

4) In accepting the deed which conveys the title to _(institution)_ subject to the life estate, _(institution)_ agrees that if Grantor is required to use the full title to this property _(institution)_ will join with him/her in the execution of whatever documents may be required to assure him/her of the full use thereof.

5) It is mutually understood and agreed by the parties to this agreement that the sole purpose of this grant is that the proceeds from the sale of the property shall be paid to _(institution)_, to be used in carrying out its corporate objectives and purposes.

IN WITNESS WHEREOF the parties have executed this agreement this _____ day of _____, 19____.

_____
Grantor

_____
(Name of Institution)

_____
By_____

Glossary of Planned Giving Terms

accountability The responsibility of an institution to provide a full public accounting of financial affairs.

accumulated deficiencies These occur during the administration of a charitable remainder unitrust (net income plus make-up) when the income actually earned by the trust is less than the percentage of the net fair market value of the trust assets. These deficiencies can be made up in future years when the trust actually earns more than the percentage of the fair market value of the trust assets.

adjusted gross income Amount of income remaining after the expenses of earning that income have been deducted.

administrator The personal representative appointed by the probate court to settle the estate of a person who dies without a will.

alumni giving program A current giving campaign directed to graduates of an educational institution.

annual fund drive The annual program for soliciting current gifts for a charity.

annuitant The person receiving annual or more frequent payments from a gift annuity.

annuity payments The annual or more frequent payment of principal and interest to an annuitant or to his or her beneficiary.

annuity reserves The required amount of money invested to guarantee the lifetime payments to the annuitant(s).

annuity trust See charitable remainder annuity trust.

appreciated property Property with a value greater than the cost basis.

assignment form (separate from certificate) A form used in transferring ownership of securities from one party to another. (The stock certificate does not have to be signed when this form is used.)

bargain sale arrangement A method whereby a person can sell appreciated property at a lower price than the fair market value to a charity, with the charity realizing the difference as a gift.

blue sky laws State laws regulating securities within that state.

board of trustees The policy-making body of a nonprofit institution.

cash surrender value The amount of money received by a policyholder from a life insurance company when the holder surrenders a policy for cash prior to the maturity date.

charitable estate planning Estate planning which includes a provision for a charitable institution to receive a portion of the person's assets.

charitable income tax deduction The amount a donor can deduct from a federal income tax return for a gift to a qualified charity.

charitable income trust See reversionary living trust.

charitable lead trust See reversionary living trust.

charitable life insurance Any type of life insurance policy which pays death proceeds or living benefits to a qualified charity.

charitable remainder annuity trust A trust created by the Tax Reform Act of 1969. It provides for a donor to transfer property to a trustee subject to the donor's right to receive a fixed percentage of the initial fair market value of the property for as long as he lives. Whatever remains in the trust at his death becomes the property of the beneficiary institution.

charitable remainder interest The amount expected to be received by a charity from a charitable remainder trust at the death of the trustor.

charitable remainder unitrust A trust created by the Tax Reform Act of 1969. It is similar to the charitable remainder annuity trust in many ways, except that the income is a percentage of the fair market value of the property determined annually.

codicil An addition or amendment to a person's will.

common disaster A situation in which husband and wife die under circumstances where it is impossible to determine who died first.

comptroller A corporation officer who is responsible for the company's financial affairs.

contract holder file The file of people who have made planned giving arrangements in favor of a charitable institution.

corpus The amount of principal in a trust.

cost basis The original cost of property plus improvements and other expenses paid by the owner during the period of ownership.

cost basis deduction The amount of deduction allowed for certain charitable gifts which do not exceed the cost of the property. (See cost basis.)

crisis mailing A solicitation for funds by direct mail which has a tone of urgency, such as, "We will have to close our doors if you don't give now."

death benefits Proceeds of a life insurance policy paid to a beneficiary of the policy at the death of the policyholder.

deferred gift A gift that is made now whereby the charitable organization does not benefit until sometime in the future according to conditions stated in a contract.

deferred payment gift annuity A gift annuity agreement issued by a qualified charity providing for payments to the beneficiary to commence at a future date and to continue for life.

direct-mail fund raising A method of soliciting gifts for a charity via mail.

director of development The officer of a charity who has responsibility for the institution's total fund development program.

dividends The amount of money paid each year on a life insurance policy or share of stock to the policyholder or the shareholder.

donor classification The separation of a donor list into groups, with divisions determined by the previous yearly amount of gifts made by each donor.

donor profile A composite profile of an institution's donors or classes of donors.

donor prospect A person believed to be a potential donor to a charity.

endowment policy A life insurance policy which provides a death benefit of the face amount should the insured die during the premium paying period. If the policyholder lives to the end of the premium paying period, he receives the face amount of the policy.

endowment A pool of property held by a charity and invested to provide an annual income for the institution.

estate analysis The process of collecting and studying data about a person's property to be used in developing an estate plan.

estate planning Planning for the management of all of an individual's assets for the benefit of this person and his or her heirs.

ex-donor file Names of donors who have ceased giving to an institution.

executor The personal representative (male) named in a will to settle the testator's estate.

executrix The personal representative (female) named in a will to settle the testator's estate.

fair market value Amount of money a willing buyer will pay a willing seller for property.

feasibility study A careful investigation of an institution's operation and structure to determine whether or not the institution should launch new programs, such as a planned giving program.

federal estate tax The tax imposed on the transfer of property to others at death.

federal gift tax The tax imposed on the transfer of property during the lifetime of the donor. This tax is paid by the donor.

federal income tax The tax on an individual's income.

fifty percent institution (A public charity is a 50 percent institution.) A person may give and deduct up to 50 percent of his adjusted gross income when giving ordinary income to a *public charity*.

five-year carry-over rule A federal income tax provision which permits a donor to carry over into the five succeeding tax years any amount of a gift which exceeds the deductible amount in the year the gift is made.

forced sale The sale of property by a person or by an estate usually at a lower than fair market price in order to obtain resources to pay legal obligations, such as estate taxes.

gift annuity agreement An agreement in which a donor makes a gift to a charity which in turn provides stipulated annual payments for life to one or two persons.

guardian A person appointed or approved by the court to look after the personal interests of another person.

inactive file Names of people who have been solicited for current gifts but have never responded.

income poor A person is said to be "income poor" when his assets are not invested in such a way as to provide adequate income.

"in-house" language Technical terms, initials, abbreviations, acronyms, etc. which are fully understood by employees, but unfamiliar to others.

in perpetuity To be held in the same form forever.

Internal Revenue Service ruling A statement defining this agency's position with respect to certain tax questions.

intestate Dying without a will.

irrevocable living trust A trust which cannot be revoked by the trustor.

joint ordinary life A life insurance policy insuring the lives of two persons.

land contract A contract between the buyer and seller of real estate providing for the payment of the unpaid balance in the transaction.

laws of descent and distribution State laws controlling distribution of property when a person dies without a will.

life estate agreement An agreement between a donor and a charity in which the donor deeds real estate to the institution but reserves the right to use or reside on the property for life.

life expectancy The actuarial estimate of the number of years a person will live from any given age.

limited payment life A life insurance policy which pays the face amount at death of the insured but requires that payments be made for 5, 10, 15, 20, or more years at a higher premium than for ordinary life policies.

liquidity Cash or readily marketable investments available to pay the cost of estate settlement.

living benefits Life insurance policy benefits paid to the policyholder while he lives.

long-term capital gains The capital appreciation realized from the sale of property (stocks, bonds, land, etc.) which the seller has owned more than twelve months.

mailing package The contents of a direct-mail solicitation, usually consisting of the carrier envelope, a letter, a brochure, a business reply envelope, and a response device.

marital deduction According to federal law, the amount of money that an individual can transfer tax free to a surviving spouse in his or her will. Currently, the marital deduction is $250,000 or one-half of the adjusted gross estate, whichever is greater.

marketing plan A comprehensive plan used in obtaining gift income from donors which has the approval of the board of trustees and is committed to writing.

matured bequest A bequest to a charity is considered "matured" when the gift is actually received by the charity.

matured charitable remainder trust A charitable remainder trust is matured when trust assets are finally delivered to the charitable institution after the death of the trustor.

memorial gift A gift to a charity in memory of a deceased person.

National Planned Giving Institute A four-week school (training division of Robert F. Sharpe & Co., Inc.) which teaches planned giving to executives of nonprofit institutions.

net income plus make-up unitrust Same as a net income unitrust except for the provision that the payments may exceed the stated percentage up to but not exceeding the amount required to make up any accumulated deficiencies for prior years, that is, years in which the trust earned less than the stated percentage. See also: charitable remainder unitrust, net income unitrust, and accumulated deficiencies.

net income unitrust A variation of the charitable remainder unitrust which provides that the trustee must pay the donor or other designated beneficiaries an amount equal to a fixed percentage of the net fair market value of the trust assets (not to be less than 5 percent) determined annually, or the actual income earned, whichever is less.

nonprofit bulk rate A special low cost mailing rate provided for nonprofit institutions by the U.S. Postal Service.

no-action letter A letter from the Securities and Exchange Commission which, in effect, means that charitable organizations can market their pooled income funds without going through the complete registration process as normally required in a securities issue.

ordinary income property Property which produces income taxed at the owner's regular income tax rate.

ordinary life Refers to an insurance policy which generally requires the policyholder to pay a level premium each year until death.

owner and beneficiary The charitable institution which has control and possession of a life insurance policy during the life of an insured person. The institution is designated to become the irrevocable charitable beneficiary at the individual's death.

parents' program A current giving campaign directed towards parents of students of an educational institution.

piggy-back mailing An additional letter, brochure, or advertising item dealing with a topic other than the primary subject of the mailing package.

planned giving The making of gifts to a charity, resulting from a planning process which considers the effects of the gift upon the donor's estate.

planned giving consultant A person who consults with the management of an institution on better ways to secure more and larger gifts on a carefully planned basis.

pledges An amount of money a person promises to give over an extended period of time.

pooled income fund A trust funded by a number of donors, each retaining an income for life. Each donor is paid a pro-rata share of the trust earnings. Each donor's portion of the principal becomes the property of the charity at the death of the donor.

powers of appointment Contractual power given by one person to another to make legal decisions on behalf of the person granting such powers.

primary beneficiary The first person named to receive the proceeds of a will

private foundation A foundation created by a person during life or at death through a will for the purpose of receiving assets to be distributed to public charities in the future.

probate The "proving" of a will. When a person dies, the will is taken to the probate court to prove that the will is indeed that person's last will and testament.

property rich A person is said to be "property rich" when he owns an adequate amount of property which produces an inadequate income.

prospect file The names of people who are motivated to give to a charity, have the money or property to give, and have confidence in the charity.

realized capital gains The amount of money received from the sale of property in excess of the original amount paid for the property.

remainderman The person or institution receiving the assets of a trust upon the death of the trustor.

residuary clause A clause in the will which bequeaths or devises property which is not specifically bequeathed or devised earlier in the will.

residue Property left for the final beneficiaries named in a will after all other bequests have been paid.

response device A coupon or card included in a direct-mail mailing package for the convenience of the recipient in requesting more information, or for indicating that a gift is being made to the charity.

retained life income plans Plans of giving which provide a gift to the charity with the donor retaining the income earned on the assets for life.

retirement income policies A life insurance policy or an annuity which pays an income for life beginning at retirement.

reversionary living trust A trust which is irrevocable for a term of years with the income being paid to the charity during this term. There is a provision for the property to revert back to the trustor at the end of the term.

revocable living trust A trust which may be revoked at any time by the trustor (with a reasonable advance warning of the intention to revoke the trust).

rights of survivorship The ownership rights held by an individual whose partner in ownership of property is no longer living.

secondary beneficiary Person named in a life insurance policy to receive the proceeds should the primary beneficiary predecease him. (May also refer to an institution.)

segregated portfolio A separate investment account covering the assets of a trust or special investment fund.

settlement costs The costs of settling an estate.

short term charitable trust See reversionary living trust.

state inheritance tax A tax on a person's right to receive property at the death of another person. The tax is paid to the state of residence of the decedent or to the state where any real property transferred is located.

straight life See ordinary life.

straight unitrust A separate trust from which a fixed percentage of the net fair market value of the trust assets, *as determined annually,* must be paid to a designated beneficiary or beneficiaries for life, or a number of years not to exceed twenty.

supplementary contract An agreement between a life insurance company and a policy beneficiary providing for the distribution of policy proceeds at a person's death or at some point during his or her life.

survivorship gift annuity A gift annuity which provides income payments to a second beneficiary surviving the first beneficiary. The payments are made to both parties while they are both alive, then to the surviving beneficiary for the remainder of his life.

suspect file The names of people who have requested information on ways to make deferred gifts to a charity.

target marketing The directing of a marketing plan to a select group of people possessing certain similar characteristics that intensify the probability of their response to the plan.

tax-exempt bonds Bonds issued by a municipality. They are free from federal and state income taxes in some states.

tax-exempt status Refers to the fact that a nonprofit corporation is exempted from paying taxes because of its charitable activities.

tax gift A gift made to a charity after tax implications have been carefully reviewed.

telephonathon A telephone campaign soliciting gifts.

telethon A television campaign for gifts.

term life A life insurance policy which is purchased for a term of years. If the person dies during this term, the beneficiary receives the face amount of the policy. The policy expires at the end of the stated number of years.

testamentary gifts Gifts made through a will.

testamentary trust A trust created by a provision in a person's will.

testator The person making a will.

third party influence The influence exercised by a third party in negotiations for a charitable gift.

tier structure Represents the way in which an income beneficiary must report for tax purposes the income generated by a charitable remainder annuity trust or unitrust. It gives the order in which the income is reported as earned by the trust. The tier is as follows: 1. ordinary income, 2. capital gains, 3. tax exempt or "other" income, 4. return of principal.

tithes The giving of 10 percent of one's income to a charitable institution. Tithing is a practice found in the Bible.

treasury regulations The regulations issued by the treasury department which interpret code sections passed by Congress.

treasury tables Actuarial, life expectancy, and other tables issued by the U.S. Treasury Department for use in calculating tax deductions for gifts made through trusts and by contract.

trustee The person or institution responsible for the administration of a trust.

trust instrument The legal document which provides operating instructions for a trustee in carrying out the terms of a trust.

trust officer The person in a trust company who is responsible for the administration of property of which the trust company is trustee.

trustor, also **grantor** The person creating a trust.

trust principal The assets of a trust.

twenty percent institution A person may give and deduct up to 20 percent of his or her adjusted gross income to a *private foundation,* which is referred to as a 20 percent institution.

unitrust See charitable remainder unitrust.

unrealized capital gain The difference between the current fair market value of some property and the original cost basis. The gain is not realized until the property is sold.

unrelated-business income rules Rules which govern the taxability of income generated from a trade or business activity unrelated to the primary purpose for which the charity gained its tax-exempt status.

whole life See ordinary life.

will A person's statement to the public regarding the disposition of his property at death.

wills clinic A presentation on wills to a group of people interested in the subject of wills.

wills emphasis program An annual direct mail solicitation emphasizing the use of the will in making charitable gifts.

Index

Mailing Address

To obtain any of the Robert F. Sharpe and Company source materials mentioned in this volume, send your specific request to:

Robert F. Sharpe and Company, Inc.
White Station Tower
5050 Poplar Avenue
Memphis, Tennessee 38157